# OUR GERMAN POLICY:

# OUR
# GERMAN
# POLICY:

*Propaganda and Culture*

By ALBERT NORMAN

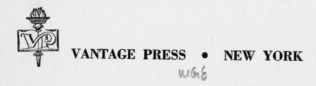

**VANTAGE PRESS • NEW YORK**

To

HILDA GORE NORMAN

# TABLE OF CONTENTS

*"If," the noble Milton said, casting his genius mind over the universe, "if this fail, the pillared firmament is rottenness."*

# PREFACE

To THE BEST OF MY KNOWLEDGE, NO GENERAL WORK has as yet been published on the subject of propaganda and culture under United States Military Government in Germany. My own interest in the topic is connected with a period in my military service. In August of 1945, when Headquarters 12th Army Group was deactivated, I was transferred to duty with the Information Control Division, Headquarters United States Forces European Theater, and placed in charge of its historical section, an unpretentious little nook in the sphere of Military Government. In that capacity I served until December 1946, having moved on with the rest of the Information Control staff from Bad Homburg near Frankfurt-am-Main, to Berlin, where we became a part of the Office of Military Government for Germany (U. S.), the American element of the Allied Control Authority.

My acquaintance with the subject, therefore, is an intimate one. At my disposal I had all the pertinent documents dealing with the media of propaganda and culture, and in this connection I had also the opportunity of consulting several important policy letters that passed between (at that time) Lt. Gen. Lucius D. Clay, the Deputy Military Governor, and Brig. Gen. Robert A. McClure, my chief. I attended the regular staff meetings, as well as the periodic meetings of leading Military Government Information Control officers in the field, where policy decisions and differences of opinion were discussed with but little restraint—to the benefit of all concerned. Numerous trips in the field to observe procedures at first hand helped in getting the "feel" of the task that lay at hand, and gained for me an experience that enriched theory with a knowledge of practice. It was an invaluable experience, now that I look back on it.

It was indeed my good fortune to have had as my superior officer General McClure, Chief of the Information Control Division at both Headquarters United States Forces European Theater and the Office of Military Government for Germany (U.S.), who in no way interfered with my work, but instead gave advice and allowed me full independence. The General imposed no restraints, other than those of propriety, which I was glad to impose on myself on my own account. It was also my good fortune to have worked under Dr. Dwight E. Lee, Chairman of the Department of History and International Relations at Clark University, who subjected me to the rigid regimen of unfettered thinking. For this I am grateful; for my own limited experience has taught me that some of the intellectual restraints imposed in some of our academic circles I would have thought of finding only in a military unit and, conversely, some of the freedoms I found in our military organization I would have thought of finding in no other place but the academic hall and the campus. I do not intend to lay this down as a general rule, but merely to cite it as a bit of my own experience.

I have made it a point in the pages that follow not to be deliberately either "objective" or "subjective." I have presented the facts as I know them—not without discrimination, of course —and wherever I thought it relevant expressed an opinion, either my own or that of another, which I credited. For I, for one, have as yet not discovered the "scientific" (or is it magic?) formula of clearly distinguishing in all cases between the objective and the subjective factors in the human—as distinguished from the *natural*—affairs of man.

To borrow a phrase: There is no fiction in this work that I know of.

ALBERT NORMAN

*Worcester, Massachusetts*

# THE APPROACH
# TO THE GERMAN QUESTION

# 1

DURING THE WAR, THE ALLIES HAD COME TO REALIZE that merely to disarm Germany militarily would not be enough. To eradicate her false ideologies of superior nationhood and the right to make war for purposes of territorial acquisition was considered just as important as curtailing Germany's physical ability to make war. Hence the Powers, each in its own zone of occupation, proceeded to place controls over the press, the publication of books and periodicals, radio broadcasting, the production and showing of films, as well as the theater and music. The underlying principle here was that by means of these controls and by the introduction into these media of a new ideological content, the mental outlook of the people would be changed, that is, the Germans would eventually be, as the term came to be applied, re-educated in accordance with democratic ways of thinking.

In analyzing the possibility of re-educating the German people, we considered it sensible to approach the problem from the point of view of whether the Germans *can* or *cannot* be re-educated. German history should, of course, to some degree, provide the answer. There are those who consider Hitler to be the only true representation of the German people's immutable character. As if no other nation had ever made war, they see in Germany nothing save "an accursed man, laden with crime, of rich talents and poor morality," [1] stalking through history to ravage the world.

---

1. G. H. Seger and S. K. Marck, *Germany: To Be or Not To Be?*, New York, 1943, pp. 56-57.

Lord Robert Vansittart, in Great Britain, and former Secretary of the Treasury Henry Morgenthau, Jr., in the United States, were the chief advocates of a school of thinking that believed that a nonwarlike Germany could be created only by subjecting her people to an absolutely complete change in her economy, by reducing her to a permanent condition of virtual pauperism and by exterminating her historical record. According to those who see only Germany's dark past, the majority of its people is more easily led astray than majorities of the peoples of other nations. It is an immutable German habit, they insist, that the majority follows where the aggressive minority leads. As one writer concludes, the Germans' respect for authority lies so deeply ingrained in their nature that "they are submissive as no other great nation." [2] Another writer sees the cause of the trouble not so much in the German people's willingness to obey but in their lack of willingness to vary in their obedience, holding obedience itself to be a commendable national trait, especially as exemplified by the British people.[3]

And Lord Vansittart? He says:"No German party, sect or organization is guiltless, and we . . . can trust nothing but an entirely renovated Germany, male and female." [4] Between Germany and humanity, he contends, there is an impassable gulf fixed; and sparing neither woman nor child he considers that one of the greatest of German problems will be "to get a new set of German mothers." [5] Not re-educating, but reforming, is what the Germans need, he contends. "They have got to become reformed characters—that is of more importance than their book learning." [6]

And Morgenthau, noting that the government of the Third Reich had left not a single medium of public information and culture unutilized for instilling in the Germans the idea of a master nation possessed of superior rights, concludes that be-

---

2. Leland Stowe, *Nazi Means War*, New York, 1934, p. 105.
3. W. F. Russell, "Teaching Germans to Teach Themselves," *Foreign Affairs*, XXVII (Oct. 1948), p. 76.
4. Lord Robert Vansittart, *Bones of Contention*, New York, 1945, p. 13.
5. *Ibid.*, p. 59.
6. *Ibid.*, p. 74.

fore that ideology can be overcome, "a whole new generation of parents must be born and raised in an entirely different atmosphere." [7]

In the United States, the Morgenthau school of thought came to dominate governmental policy, as it was adopted by President Franklin D. Roosevelt. In September of 1944 the President asked Morgenthau to outline for him a program for the treatment of Germany after her defeat, wishing to take such a document to the Quebec Conference, which was soon to be held.[8] In his memorandum to Roosevelt, styled "a program to prevent Germany from starting a World War III," Morgenthau laid down the basic postulate that as long as Germany had her heavy industry the possibility of starting a new war would always exist. He therefore proposed Germany's complete deindustrialization and her turning into a pastoral country. Once she no longer had the means to wage war, the new educational task could begin. Morgenthau therefore proposed that as soon as the Allied armies stepped onto German soil, all German newspapers, magazines, radio stations, motion pictures, theatrical life, and like activities should be discontinued until adequate controls could be established. The controls were to insure an end to the teaching of the Nazi creed and to the dissemination of warlike ideas. Highly qualified Allied personnel were to do this. But as far as re-education was concerned, those Germans who had never fallen prey to National Socialist ideology would have to shoulder the burden.

Agreed to at Quebec, the Morgenthau principles were, in their broad outline, incorporated in the Yalta Agreement of February 11, 1945.[9] They also determined the philosophy of the first United States Government directive regarding the military government of Germany, issued April 26, 1945 by the Joint Chiefs of Staff as document JCS 1067/6 to the Commander-in-

---

7. Henry Morgenthau, Jr., *Germany is Our Problem,* New York and London, 1945, p. 150.
8. *Ibid.,* p. xi.
9. For text of Yalta Agreement see Gustav Stolper, *German Realities, New* York, 1948, pp. 261-63.

( 11 )

Chief of the United States forces of occupation.[10] The basic principles of Morgenthau's program thus came to represent the official position of the United States Government.[11] It is our "inflexible purpose," stated the Yalta communique, "to destroy German militarism and Nazism" and to "remove all the Nazi and militarist influences . . . from the cultural and economic life of the German people." But since these influences could in part only be removed by removing the people who exerted them, the policy of denazification was introduced as a preliminary step, in both the rebuilding of Germany's social structure and in her eventual ideological reorientation. However, the policy of denazification soon involved the policy-makers in a most complex contradiction. They had made war not only on the Nazi government (as President Wilson had on the Kaiser's government) but on the whole German people—on the apparently new theory of "collective guilt."

JCS 1067/6 directed the American Commander to bring home to all Germans, without distinction, the idea that they "cannot escape responsibility" for what they had brought upon themselves. All personal contact and fraternization of the occupation forces with the German population was to be strongly discouraged. However, in the fact that the victors set out to denazify the government apparatus, thereby differentiating between "guilty" and "innocent," there was inherent a refutation of their own theory of "collective guilt" of the whole German people, which JCS 1067/6 recognized.

Furthermore, although the principal sources of the Hitler dictatorship were primarily economic, the Commander-in-Chief of the American occupation forces was directed "to take no steps looking toward the economic rehabilitation of Germany, or designed to maintain or strengthen the German economy." Yet, he was under instructions, contained in the same basic policy document, to create conditions under which democracy and the objective of preventing Germany "from ever again be-

10. For text of JCS 1067/6 see Stolper, pp. 273-93 and James K. Pollock, *Germany Under Occupation*, Ann Arbor, Mich., 1947, pp. 100-15.
11. Morgenthau, op. cit., p. xii.

coming a threat to the peace of the world" could be realized. In the sphere of public education the propagation of Nazi, militaristic and pan-German doctrines was prohibited, but within these specified limitations, and to the extent necessary to safeguard military interests, freedom of speech and press was permitted.

Morgenthau's basic plan of punishing Germany economically and of keeping her in a state of pauperism, which, as we have seen, forms the underlying concept of JCS 1067/6, was in part incorporated in the Potsdam Agreement of August 1945, which formulated general occupation policy for the whole of Germany. The average living standard called for in that Agreement is a very low one, scarcely the standard on which a democratic form of government and democratic ways of thinking can be built up. None the less, the Potsdam Agreement, in the same breath—though in evident contradiction—goes on to declare one of the purposes of the occupation to be the reconstruction of German life along democratic lines.

It was not until experience—and some wisdom—began to play its modest role in the approach to the German problem that a new military government policy directive was issued to the American Commander-in-Chief and Military Governor in Germany, on July 15, 1947, correctly appraising the economic, political, and re-educational problem.[12] It was there at last recognized that a new, democratic life could come to Germany only if "resting on a substantial basis of economic well-being," which would lead to tranquillity within the country and contribute "to the spirit of peace among nations."

The task in Germany, therefore, correctly came to be thought of as primarily one of laying the economic foundation of a sound German democracy and of ideological reorientation. The economic conditions, it was recognized, had first to be created before there could be any hope of a successful political and educational reorientation in Germany. At last, solid ration-

---

12. For the text of Joint Chiefs of Staff Directive of July 15, 1947, which replaced JCS 1067/6, see Stolper, pp. 312-25, and H. Price and C. E. Schorske, *The Problem of Germany*, New York, 1947, pp. 149-61.

al thinking—or plain common sense—was restored to its proper place in our political actions.

Several agencies carried on the planning for military government in the American zone of Germany. Basic policy decisions were made in Washington. Less important policies were drawn up at Headquarters United States Forces European Theater and the Office of Military Government for Germany (U.S.), both of which were under the command of the Commander-in-Chief of the American Armed Forces in Europe. This dual —and never clearly defined—responsibility as between Washington and the European Theater and the ill-defined spheres of responsibility between the Department of State and War Department led to considerable uncertainty in planning and to conclusions that were not thoroughly thought out.[13]

Thus the early planning days were not happy ones: there was no centralized responsibility; no full maturity of approach as to our general obligations both in Germany and Europe as a whole; no counterweight to the public's clamor for our troops to come home. It was evident to anyone in the European Theater in the immediate posthostilities period, and especially to those on the staff of Military Government in Germany that, as one writer states, our officials failed to learn the lessons provided by the occupation of the Rhineland after the First World War.[14]

On top of that, even the most technically competent of American officials were considerably lacking in political awareness, and it was not uncommon "for problems to be considered with little or no reference to their political implications." [15]

Early in the occupation of Germany, our policy prohibited the Germans from engaging in political activities. It also stressed, in press and on the radio operated by the United States Army that the idea of the collective guilt of the German people

13. For an able survey of Military Government functions and organization, see Harold Zink, *American Military Government in Germany*, New York, 1947.
14. Ernest Fraenkel, *Military Occupation and the Rule of Law*, New York and London, 1947, p. 225.
15. Harold Zink, "A Political Scientist Looks at Military Government in the European Theater of Operations," *The American Political Science Review*, XL (December 1946), p. 1107.

for the inhumanities of the Nazi regime and its war of aggression was a necessary prerequisite to any long-term re-education of the Germans. This policy had the reverse effect upon the Germans from the one contemplated by the United States Government, especially from the one contemplated by the Morgenthau school of policy-makers. Instead of accepting individual responsibility for the misdeeds of the National Socialist Party and Government, the traditionally politically inactive sections of the population tended to sink more deeply into inactivity, and blame, especially for concentration camp atrocities, was shunted to those directly responsible for them—the top Nazi Party leaders. Collective guilt was never accepted. The efforts on our part "to arouse a sense of collective responsibility" for the Nazi crimes, in the words of Brig. Gen. Robert A. McClure, head of American Military Government's information and culture program "never took root." [16]

The program of re-education of the German people, in order to succeed, had, therefore, to take on a different tenor. The theme that every German—whether man, woman, or child, of whatever political affiliation, or no affiliation—was personally responsible for the crimes of the Nazi regime was, in January of 1946, officially abandoned and a position taken which was the very reverse of it. The media of information and cultural dissemination began to give prominence to evidence of resistance under the Nazi regime and to make a distinction between individuals who had planned and carried out the systematic crimes of the Nazis and those who had been anti-Nazi and pro-democratic and constituted the Allies' main hope of creating a peaceful Germany. A new policy directive of the Office of Military Government for Germany (U.S.), the top American Military Government headquarters, clearly stressed that simultaneously with eradicating Nazi ideology, the formation of democratic political parties should be encouraged, as well as labor unions and similar organizations. All Germans were not to be con-

---

16. Gladwin Hill, "Allied-Soviet Unity Lacking on Germans' Re-education," *New York Times*, May 26, 1945.

demned; and those in democratic political and trade union activity, in positions of leadership on newspapers and periodicals, in universities and church, and in youth organizations were to be encouraged to train themselves for a democratic Germany. The occupation forces were to guide particularly the youth, which was confused and bewildered, and unwilling to follow in the footsteps of its elders. Into this amorphous situation the United States was to endeavor to stimulate democratic ideology.

And yet, in one very important respect American re-education policy continued unchanged—it continued to remain negative. The position of Military Government was to be that of guardian, prohibiting and admonishing, rather than that of an instructor, teaching and pointing out the way.

This attitude was incorporated in the Potsdam Agreement,[17] which, with certain omissions and minor modifications, had written into it the substance of JCS 1067/6 with regard to re-education. The Agreement states briefly that the re-education of the Germans "shall be so controlled as completely to eliminate Nazi and militarist doctrines and to make possible the successful development of democratic ideas," and that "subject to the necessity for maintaining military security, freedom of speech, press, and religion shall be permitted." The responsibility of the victorious powers was thus declared to be first and foremost a negative one. From the very beginning, American policy considered it unwise for the Allies to attempt the direct re-education of the Germans. The uncertainty of the length of the occupation, the comparative absence of planning along those lines, the anxiety at the end of hostilities "to close out" and "to go home" were important factors in determining our attitude toward the question of the mass cultural media in the United States zone of occupation. The conviction became firmly fixed that German re-education would have to be accomplished in the final analysis by the Germans themselves.

Some Military Government officials, who *had* given thought to long-range problems of re-education, felt that the Potsdam

17. For text of Potsdam Agreement, *see* Morgenthau, op. cit., pp. 213-29.

Agreement did suggest a positive line of action and they urged a positive re-educational program. The Three Power Agreement did speak of making "possible the successful development of democratic ideas," and in this phrase they saw a recognition of the fact that there first must be created the prerequisites upon which democratic ideas could grow. Gradually, cognizance was taken of the simple political truism that the reforming of the way of thinking of a populous, highly industrialized, and scientifically advanced nation could not be conducted in a vacuum, but must be conducted on the basis of the closest association of ideology and the economic, political, and social structure of the country. No thoughtful observer could fail to see that re-education of the German people—positive, long-range re-education, that is, not merely the restrictive, "controlling" type of Military Government's—could be effective only as an integral part of a comprehensive program for German economic and political re-habilitation. The Vansittart and Morgenthau plans of converting Germany into a pauperized pastoral state and, at the same time, re-educating the people to democracy were mutually contradictory—mutually exclusive—aims. The former could never have led to the latter; it led straight to the Germany of the 1930's—desperation, confusion, National Socialism, dictatorship, war. The Morgenthau plan had to be discarded.

The first gun in a revisionist German policy fired on the highest political level, and marking a break with the basic philosophy underlying the Morgenthau Memorandum to President Roosevelt, the Yalta Agreement, JCS 1067/6, and to a degree, Potsdam, came from Secretary of State James F. Byrnes in his speech of September 6, 1946, at Stuttgart, Germany. "The American people," the Secretary of State said, "have long since ceased to talk of a hard or a soft peace for Germany . . . We will oppose harsh and vengeful measures which obstruct an effective peace." He then went on to affirm that the American Government and people "want to help the German people to win their way back to an honorable place among the free and peace-loving nations of the world," to which end he pledged the support of the United States in denazifying Germany and in placing ever greater reliance on anti-Nazi Germans. An occupation army, however well motivated and disciplined, the Secretary of State went on to say, is not in the long run the most reliable guardian of another country's democracy. Germans tested in their devotion to dramatic ideals and methods should form the mainstay of American Military Government. Thus, Military Government officials were encouraged in the hope that the existing measures taken by means of the mass media of cultural dissemination to introduce the best ideological features in American and Western European life would be at least continued, if not expanded. The existing official American media in the German language, such as the newspaper *Neue Zeitung*, the periodicals *Auslese* and *Heute*, and the Anglo-American newsreel, were assured a new lease on life.[18]

And a year later, in July 1947, the new policy approach to the German question was finally "recognized," receiving the official stamp of approval in the form of the new Joint Chiefs of Staff directive to the American Commander-in-Chief and Military Governor in the United States zone of Germany, General Lucius D. Clay. Long experience in the field, coupled with some solid political and sociological planning on the "lower levels" of occupation planning (which Morgenthau, in 1944, pooh-poohed) had at last created a realistic American Military Government policy. Technically, JCS 1067/6 was in force from April 1945 to July 1947. Actually, its "revenge" provisions and its objective of "undoing" things rather than doing something positive in bringing Germany back to the much-talked-of "family of democratic and peace-loving nations" had to be abandoned, one by one, as unworkable, if not officially abandoned as based on the wrong ideological conclusions. The cultural reorientation of the Germans in the United States areas of occupation, according to the new directive, was henceforth to be conducted in such a way as to *assist* the pro-democratic Germans in the development of the media of public education.

---

18. For detailed discussion, see Chapters III, IV, V.

# POLICIES OF AMERICAN
# MILITARY GOVERNMENT

## 2

SHORT-RANGE POLICIES ON REORIENTATION TO BE AP-
plied in the United States areas of occupation were formulated
by the Information Control Division at Headquarters United
States Forces European Theater, located in Bad Homburg, and
after the early spring of 1946 at the Office of Military Government for Germany (U.S.), in Berlin, to which the Control
Division was transferred. These policies were based on broad
political directives from the Office of War Information,[1] whose
main function consisted of formulating educational and cultural
programs designed to develop an understanding of the war
policies and aims of the United States, to be carried out through
the use of the press, radio, motion pictures, and other facilities.
The new federal agency also served as an agency of contact for
the radio broadcasting and motion picture industries and for
novelists and playwrights.

Since the mass media of cultural dissemination in Germany
were controlled in order to further military and political objectives, as formulated by the Joint Chiefs of Staff and the

---

1. The Office of War Information was created on June 13, 1942 by
Executive Order 9182, which consolidated certain war information
functions carried out by several government agencies, such as the Office of Facts and Figures and the Office of Government Reports. It was
abolished on August 31, 1945 by Executive Order 9608 and its functions
transferred to the Interim International Information Service of the
Department of State. *See Federal Register*, VII (June 16, 1942), pp.
4468-69; and X (September 1, 1945), p. 11223.

American Military Governor,[2] a working agreement was entered into by Elmer Davis, Director of the Office of War Information, and Brig. Gen. Robert A. McClure, Chief of the Information Control Division, designed to prevent conflicting points of view and to establish a smooth-working relationship on practical issues bound to arise in the making of policy and its application.

The execution of policy was divided into three phases. The first phase called for the total prohibition of German public education and cultural media; the second, for the employment of official ("overt," as it was then called) American educational services and the simultaneous searching out of anti-Nazi Germans who could be trusted to re-establish indigenous media under Military Government supervision; and the third phase, for the gradual transition to complete control of the cultural media by the Germans themselves, under the supervision of the Military Government authorities on the highest level only.

In the first phase, following closely upon the heels of the victorious armies, Military Government law provided the authority for the outlawing of the Nazi propaganda organization. The laws prohibited any German, of any political shading whatsoever, from publishing papers, books and periodicals, radio broadcasting, the showing of motion pictures, the giving of theatrical and operatic performances, and the conducting of concerts; they also empowered the occupation forces to remove from their positions all persons who had fashioned National Socialist ideology. To fill the void created by the outlawry of the highly centralized Nazi propaganda machine and by the destruction of physical plant facilities as a result of the fighting, the two most important public education media—newspapers and radio—were, therefore, operated by the United States

---

2. The Commander-in-Chief of American forces of occupation was by virtue of his military position also Military Governor. General of the Army Dwight D. Eisenhower and after him (since November 1945) Gen. Joseph T. McNarney entrusted practically all of their military government responsibilities to Lt. Gen. Lucius D. Clay, who, as Deputy Military Governor, was in direct command of the Office of Military Government for Germany (U.S.), in Berlin, the American element of the Allied Control Authority. It was not until March 1947 that General Clay became Commander-in-Chief as well as Military Governor.

Army itself. A number of German newspapers were published by the Army and distributed through military channels. Radio stations that had been quickly restored began to operate inside Germany as stations of Military Government. What was said in press and radio, then, was the responsibility solely of the army of occupation. German technical personnel was, however, employed to the fullest possible extent, while preparations were in progress for the establishment of new, democratic, cultural services, controlled by Germans who had been approved by Military Government, but who were closely supervised and watched. Press, publications, and film, theater, and music officers searched for politically reliable and professionally qualified men. Suitable individuals were issued Military Government licenses to publish newspapers, books, and magazines; to direct and stage theatrical performances, and to organize symphonic concerts. Owners of bookshops and distributors of newspapers and periodicals were allowed to engage in business as soon as they were found to be politically unobjectionable and had registered their business with Military Government of their area. At the same time, German editors, whose political backgrounds had been thoroughly investigated and who proved acceptable, were added to the staffs of the radio stations operated by Military Government.

Military Government proceeded slowly in licensing Germans to assume important positions in the field of the mass education media because of the necessity of finding men who were completely reliable and who were suited to play a positive part in the democratic reorientation of Germany. Political qualifications demanded of the Germans were more rigorous than in some other fields of public life, and investigations were exhaustive. Positive anti-Nazis were sought, rather than mere non-Nazis, to operate the public education media.[3] Germans chosen for policy, editorial, and certain executive positions had not only to be technically qualified but had to have harbored demo-

---

3. Office of Military Government for Germany (U.S.), *Monthly Report of the Military Governor, U. S. Zone, Information Control*, No. 13, August 20, 1946, p. 2, hereafter referred to as Report of the Military Governor.

cratic ideals, which were defined as the belief in freedom of speech, religion, and thought; faith in the dignity of the indivual against the pre-eminence of the state; and a conviction that crimes against civilized standards of morals and humanity are as intolerable when committed in the name of the state as when committed by a private citizen. Leading newspaper and magazine publishers, editors, radio men, and theatrical producers were usually chosen, therefore, from among the ranks of those who had resisted National Socialism to the point where they were imprisoned or at least had become known in their communities as opponents of the Nazi regime.

The initial prohibition of the operation of German information services was decreed by Military Government Law 191, in January 1945. It exempted television broadcasts and the sale and distribution of sound recordings. The law was later amended to prohibit the hitherto exempted prohibitions, and was promulgated, in June, as Military Government Law 191, Amended (1). The procedure by which Germans were allowed to operate public education services on their own behalf, under Military Government supervision, was laid down in Information Control Regulation No. 1. A German national who wished to engage in an enterprise that involved the creation of ideology or the employment of media of ideological dissemination (newspapers, book publishing, stage shows, etc.) had to apply to Military Government of his area for a license. After thorough investigation, if the license were granted, he could legally engage in his business. In those cases where a license was not required, the German wishing to go into business in any of the media of public education had to register with the local Military Government office. This included such people as book and news dealers, motion picture theater owners, printers, sheet music dealers, individual artists, and the like. Licenses were issued only to a "natural" person or to several "natural" persons associated together; corporations or associations were ruled out. This was done with the idea in mind of being able to hold individuals responsible for any breach of Military Government law.

Frequently, the use of German property had to be acquired

for the operation of the cultural media. Property and equipment of the defunct German state and of the Nazi party and its affiliates was confiscated without payment of any kind; other property was subject to reimbursement at some future date. Although, generally, tangible and intangible wealth was confiscated or requisitioned by the occupation forces for their own use, in the public education media they were confiscated or requisitioned for Germans holding Military Government licenses. Owing to the extensive destruction of physical plant and equipment, it was necessary for Military Government to provide newspaper publishers and theatrical producers with whatever facilities it was capable of mustering.

However, the licensee thus put up in business was not allowed to make a windfall gain from his enterprise. He was required to pay a fair rental for the use of nonconsumable property, such as buildings and presses, and for consumables, such as newsprint and ink. Such payments were deposited by the German businessman in a special blocked account in the nearest branch of the Reichsbank. The account could be "unblocked" only by permission of the Information Control Division of the Office of Military Government for Germany (U. S.).

The first in a series of directives which laid down the editorial policy for the official United States Army newspapers published for the Germans, and for radio broadcasts, was issued in May 1945. Its aim was to inform the Germans of the military and economic objectives of the occupation and to develop in them a deepening sense of acquiescence to occupation authority. As for ideological reorientation, the presenting of facts of war guilt and of the true system of National Socialism and its atrocities were the only things permitted. These early steps in the direction of influencing German thinking aimed at arousing in the populace a sense of collective responsibility for Nazi crimes. But very soon afterwards the theme was changed, the active guilt of the criminal being differentiated clearly from the passive guilt of the people as a whole. There had taken place, then, a metamorphosis—from the theme of active collective

guilt to the theme of passive collective guilt, officially introduced, as previously mentioned, in January 1946.[4]

Gradually, the process of returning the cultural media to
the Germans was begun. The Army-published newspapers were
one by one discontinued, and first steps taken to put into
practice the policy of selecting and licensing Germans to start
publishing their own newspapers in what was hoped would
subsequently become an independent democratic press. Signs
had come to the fore to indicate in a number of ways that
desirable groups of potential German licensees were emerging
in various parts of the United States areas of occupation and
the time had ripened when practical steps could be taken in
applying the policy of letting the Germans run their own media
of information and culture. Germans, rather than the Military
Government authorities, were now to speak to Germans. They
were themselves to provide a corrective to the unhealthy state
of mind of the German population, which combined bewilder-
ment and political apathy with a general non-recognition of war
guilt (either active or passive) and guilt for crimes committed
by the Nazi government. It had become sufficiently clear that
the Allies' attempts through their own newspapers and radio
broadcasts to create a mentality of war guilt had proved a
failure.

In selecting potential licensees, particularly as far as large
cities were concerned, groups of Germans were considered pref-
erable to a single individual, since it was felt that the licensing
of a single individual in a large community would be resented
by equally reputable leaders and sections of the community with
differing religious or political beliefs. When licensed, each
group had to be representative of the main anti-Nazi elements
in the community, but the licensees were not allowed to consider themselves as spokesmen for any particular political party
or religious belief. It was the thought of Military Government
that various beliefs on a newspaper, for example, would balance
each other to produce a paper politically of the center. Another

---

4. *See* p. 14.

important factor was the constant serious shortage of newsprint, which made it impossible to license more than one newspaper in any one city.

The mass education media were begun to be turned over to the Germans late in July 1945, and the beginning was made with the press when the first license to publish a newspaper— the *Frankfurter Rundschau*—was issued on the 31st of the month. Soon, German publishers, who had been issued Military Government licenses, began to dominate the book and periodicals field, although limited paper stocks kept the output small. More and more radio functions were entrusted to German personnel, with the result that in the autumn of 1946 American Military Government had only a general supervisory function in the broadcasting stations, and nearly all department heads were German. The same development occurred in the case of *DANA* (*Deutsche Allgemeine Nachrichten Agentur*), the German news service. Founded by Military Government to supply factual news to the licensed German press, *DANA* had in a comparatively short time become an almost completely German enterprise, with only a very few Military Government supervisors and reporters on its staff.[5]

When operation of most of the public education and culture media began to be turned over to the Germans, greater latitude was given the licensees for the expression of opinion. Under the terms of the Potsdam Agreement of August 2, 1945, freedom of expression was encouraged, subject to the necessity for preventing Nazi propaganda and for maintaining military security. This meant that all types of news and editorials could be permitted as long as they did not violate the stipulated restrictions. Thus, in September, Military Government gave the German licensees a free hand to discuss local, regional, or national issues and to engage in political activities as a step in the direction to full democratic freedom. Newspapers, radio commentators, and actors were encouraged to exercise full rights of political and social evaluation and criticism. They still could not, however,

---

5. *Report of the Military Governor*, op. cit.

( 25 )

criticize announced Military Government policies and Allied officials; nor could they use their media to create division among the Allies or to sow disrespect for the United Nations. Prepublication scrutiny of the press ceased, except where it was required to the safeguarding of military intelligence and the lives and property of occupying forces. In its stead, postpublication scrutiny was instituted.

As a corollary to the increased freedom of expression granted the Germans, new sources of news material were opened to them. Files of the leading American news agencies were made available to the German press; copyrights of American books were sold to German publishers; American and other foreign plays were brought to the stage; and foreign music scores were imported for the use of orchestras. American libraries—or information centers, as they were called—were opened to the public in the major cities, providing a variety of American and foreign material to students, research workers, and writers. In political content, the course in the reorientation of Germany pursued by the United States was a "middle" course. It was a policy repeatedly emphasized by General McClure, who was in direct charge of the program; had the sanction of Assistant Secretary of State William Benton;[6] and was carried out in practice.

The only literature political parties were allowed to publish was handbills and posters. They were at the same time granted a limited opportunity to make use of the press—though not to have newspapers of their own. The licensed German press was instructed by Military Government to give a certain amount of space to all authorized political parties. The handbills and posters had to be printed in a registered printing shop and copies filed with Military Government before distribution. Owing to the critical shortage of newsprint and the demands made on the limited supply by newspaper and book publishers, each political party was authorized to produce handbills not in excess

---

6. The author's notes, taken at the staff meeting of the Information Control Division, USFET, November 18, 1945 at Bad Homburg, Germany. The meeting was attended by Asst. Sec. of State William Benton.

of one for every ten persons in its area in any one month and posters not in excess of one for every hundred people.

On the all-important question of how soon to turn over the information and cultural media to the Germans and the degree of control to be exercised by Military Government, there developed a considerable difference of opinion in high official quarters in Germany. General McClure, late in 1945, urged a slow and cautious policy, especially in view of the strong unofficial undercurrent to "close out." He believed that the function of licensing should be exercised by Military Government personnel as long as it was necessary and not turned over to German governmental agencies which, he feared, might establish local ministries of propaganda and thereby prevent free cultural media from developing. When licensing should prove necessary no longer, General McClure held, it should then be abolished altogether.[7]

But not so General Clay. The Deputy Military Governor was not at all like-minded. He held that Military Government control in the form of granting and withholding licenses should limit itself to the protection of the public against "fraudulent enterprises" and to the prevention of "malicious information" being circulated. "By the continued selection of German personnel, a healthy press cannot be established and I believe that the actions of Military Government at the earliest possible date should be restricted to disapproval of personnel rather than to their selection," wrote General Clay. This procedure, he opined, would convince the German people of the sincerity of the United States in its belief in democratic processes. Whereas General McClure wanted Military Government to teach and point out to the Germans what they must do, General Clay wanted to restrict it to listing those things which the Germans must not do, leaving the remainder of the field free.[8]

"In the interim, I would like for you to plan along the lines I have indicated," was General Clay's instructions to his

---

7. Brig. Gen. Robert A. McClure to Lt. Gen. Lucius D. Clay, November 23, 1945.
8. General Clay to Gen. McClure, December 14, 1945.

Information Control chief. And he proceeded to lay down basic Military Government policy for guiding the reorientation of German thinking for the period immediately lying ahead:[9]

(1) Responsibility for information service activities to be turned over to the Germans as rapidly as possible; (2) in press matters, the eventual objective to be that of allowing political parties to publish their own organs in place of the extant temporary expedient of allowing only selected individuals to publish; (3) to maintain in Germany the official United States Government publications for the direct communication of the American point of view on national and international questions— the newspaper *Die Neue Zeitung*, and the periodicals *Amerikanische Rundschau* and *Heute*; (4) to continue the British-American newsreel *Welt im Film* and the periodical *Neue Auslese*; (5) and to continue for an indefinite period of time to exercise policy control over German radio broadcasting.

In line with General Clay's policy, therefore, an advance in the granting of complete freedom of expression in Germany was taken later in the year, when German newspapers were granted permission to carry factual accounts of world events as freely as the press of other free nations. Although Nazi and militarist propaganda and malicious material was still banned, the new ruling did not exclude legitimate news stories. This may not, at first sight, appear as much of a step forward, based on American and Western European standards. But from the point of view of the Germans and of Military Government it was not an inconsequential move in the right direction. Under policy regulations in effect since early 1945, the Germans could neither print material unfavorable to Military Government nor say anything critical of any of the United Nations. Nor could they criticize important political figures. The effect of these regulations was to prohibit the publication of bona fide and important news in some cases. Under the new regulation, these restrictions were

---

9. General Clay to General McClure, January 17, 1946.

removed, and the German cultural services were, in addition, permitted to quote from non-German newspapers, magazines, and broadcasts—something they could not do before—subject only to copyright restrictions. Non-German commercial news agencies were allowed to enter Germany and to make contracts with licensed newspapers by special permission of the United States Treasury, a procedure made necessary by the existence of the wartime Trading with the Enemy Act. Material that was thought likely to constitute malicious writing was the "slanting" of headlines and the featuring of news that told only half a story and the suppression of the other half. A newspaper, for example, that combed world news files for items unfavorable to one of the Powers occupying Germany, and deliberately failed to print the news that was favorable to that Power was considered as subject to disciplinary action by Military Government.

Up to the time of the introduction of this policy change, the record of nearly all licensees under American jurisdiction had been good, and Military Government felt confident that the Germans responsible for the media of public education would use the new freedom that was granted them to give better and fuller news and to hasten the reintegration of at least Western Germany into what has come to be called the "family of nations."

It was the belief of Military Government policy-makers in Germany that a free exchange of ideas and opinions was basic to the establishment in the American areas of occupation of a democratic society. To this end it was the purpose of the United States Government to allow increasing freedoms and responsibilities in the cultural and information media at such time and in such measure as those responsible for the press, the publishing business, radio, the motion picture industry, the theater, and music gave evidence of their readiness and fitness to assume them. The length of the phases through which the cultural media would have to pass in order to be eligible for complete freedom depended, therefore, in the view of the United States, on the conduct of those Germans selected to engage in the cultural services. Each licensee was viewed as a trustee for a vital part of Germany's future—for that part of her future, at least, over which the United States exercised direct control and influence.

# THE EMERGENCE
# OF AN INDIGENOUS PRESS

# 3

SINCE THE NEWSPAPER RANKS FIRST AMONG PROPAGANDA
and public education media, the American and British Armies,
as they entered Germany, brought with them German newspapers, published by Supreme Headquarters, Allied Expeditionary Force, which they distributed to the civilian population.
When, in July 1945, Germany was partitioned into zones of
occupation, Headquarters United States Forces European
Theater took over this responsibility in the American zone of
occupation and sector of Berlin. Newspapers were published
as official organs of the occupying forces. They numbered nine
in July, had a combined circulation of close to 3,500,000,
and were spread over cities such as Heidelberg, Bremen,
Straubing, Kassel, Augsburg, Frankfurt, Bamberg, Munich, and
Berlin.[1] Gradually, the publication of these papers was discontinued and the field given over to newspapers published by Germans who were issued licenses for that purpose by Military
Government. Although this procedure was regarded by some
officials as premature, holding that there still was a place for regional Military Government newspapers to present to the German people the American point of view on current problems,
even if German newspapers were desirable at the same time,
the general policy that was practiced was to turn such activi-

---

1. The names of the newspapers were as follows: *Allgemeine Zeitung,
   Augsburger Zeitung, Bayrische Landeszeitung, Frankfurter Presse, Hes-
   siche Post, Munchener Zeitung, Regensburger Post, Süddeutsche Würt-
   temberger,* and *Weser Bote.*

ties over to the Germans as soon as possible. Thus, by November 1945, all but one of the official Military Government newspapers in the German language, *Die Neue Zeitung*, had ceased publication and their place taken by the indigenous licensed press.

The official press had filled the gap created by Military Government Law 191 and had kept the population informed of world and local events as well as of essential occupation policies. It had also served as a model of the type of newspaper Military Government wished to see the Germans introduce themselves, that is, a newspaper not given over to too much editorializing, but to straightforward news reporting, with emphasis on international rather than provincial news. In pre-Hitler days it was the political editorial, not the highlights of the news, that had occupied the most prominent place in a German newspaper.[2]

Unlike the practice in the Second World War, during the First World War the German press was not outlawed, and there was no such thing as official Military Government newspapers. There also was no such thing as selecting, approving, and licensing newspaper publishers, and there had never arisen the question of the "re-education" of the German people. Only censorship had to be resorted to—for a time. Some propaganda and a tendency to criticize occupation procedures in the district occupied by American troops had brought on General Pershing's press order of December 1918, checking this criticism.[3] However, relations between the American military authorities and the German press were, on the whole, so correct, that encounters over the appearance of subject matter reflecting on occupation policy were very rare.[4]

The situation after World War II, as we have already shown, was quite different. A complicated and long-drawn-out system of physically locating, investigating, and licensing pro-democratic, professionally qualified Germans had to be re-

---

2. Felix E. Hirsch, "The German Press, Yesterday and Tomorrow," *Current History*, IX (August 1945), p. 105.
3. *New York Times*, December 21, 1918, p. 35.
4. W. F. Sollmann, "The German Press After V-Day," *The Public Opinion Quarterly*, VIII (1944-45), p. 541.

sorted to. These Germans then had to be provided with buildings, presses, newsprint, and other materials essential to newspaper publishing.

During the first months of the occupation of Germany, Headquarters United States Forces European Theater reserved to itself the exclusive right to grant licenses to applicants recommended by the lower echelons of Military Government working in the sphere of the cultural media. Once the lower echelons had demonstrated their ability to apply policies scrupulously, they were given permission to grant licenses on their own authority, with the single stipulation that cities selected for the publication of newspapers would have to be approved by Theater Headquarters and that no more than one newspaper would be licensed in any one city.

The licensed publisher or publishers were required to form a business corporation in accordance with the terms of German law and statutes as approved by Military Government. Only publishers holding licenses could be owners and partners of a business corporation and the only types of corporations permitted in the newspaper business were sole ownership, open partnership, and limited and mixed-limited liability corporations. The business contracts and any later changes and amendments had to be approved by Military Government, and in order to safeguard the ownership of a newspaper as an enterprise of licensees, the business contract had to provide that a publisher whose license was revoked or who withdrew voluntarily as a licensee would immediately cease to be a partner in the enterprise. Military Government also reserved to itself the right to inspect the books, files, inventories, stockpiles, etc., of licensed newspapers to assure their operation on safe financial principles.

The first German newspaper to be published in the United States zone of occupation was the *Frankfurter Rundschau*, which appeared on July 31, 1945. Seven men, representing various shades of political thought, were made jointly responsible for its publication and an initial circulation of almost half a million copies enabled it to cover a large part of Hesse. The *Rundschau*

( 33 )

was well received by the public. The difficulties in getting out a newspaper under the handicap of shortages was recognized by all and the general reaction was that it was good to have a really German newspaper again.

Newspapers in other large cities followed the *Frankfurter Rundschau* during the next few months, such as the *Rhein-Neckar Zeitung* in Heidelberg, on September 6; the *Marburger Presse*, on the 15th; the *Stuttgarter Zeitung*, two days later; and the *Weser Kurier*, in Bremen, the same day. During the same month appeared the *Hessische Nachrichten*, in Kassel, and the *Wiesbadener Kurier*. In Munich appeared the *Suddeutsche Zeitung*; in Garmisch-Partenkirchen, the *Hochland Bote;* and in Nurnberg the *Nurnberger Nachrichten*. Other newspapers were licensed in Hof, the "border town" on the American-Russian boundary in Upper Franconia, in Augsburg, Darmstadt, and Regensberg.[5]

These newspapers were started initially with large circulations. As others were started in smaller centers, the authorized areas of circulation and the total circulation of nearby papers were generally reduced. The total circulation of the licensed press therefore remained fairly constant at approximately four million by late 1946, although at that time 38 newspapers were appearing in the American zone of occupation, including the Bremen enclave and the American sector of Berlin.[6] In the latter city, the newspaper licensed by American Military Government was *Der Tagesspiegel*, founded on September 27, 1945, and a frequent target for Berlin's Soviet-sponsored press. Because of the serious shortage of newsprint, newspapers appeared only twice or thrice weekly on designated days in editions of from four to six pages. The only exception to this rule was *Der Tagesspiegel*, which appeared six times weekly, in view of the political importance of the former German capital in the contest of influence between the Soviet Union and the Western Powers over the allegiance of its people.

5. ICD/USFET, *News of Germany*, September 4, 18, 20, 1945.
6. *Report of the Military Governor*, op. cit., p. 3.

The publication of newspapers on a twice- and thrice-weekly basis was necessitated by one constant factor: the acute newsprint shortage. Few problems were more complex and more difficult of solution. It figured prominently in every attempt to increase the circulation of newspapers as well as the volume of book publication. Until late in 1945, Military Government depended for its paper supply chiefly on stocks of German finished paper found in warehouses in the American zone of occupation. After that, however, a systematic method of making quarterly estimates of newsprint requirements was put into effect, Bavaria receiving some 1,500 tons, Hesse some 1,300, and Wurttemberg-Baden something like 900 tons. In turn, each newspaper received an allocation from the press control officer of Military Government of the *Land* in which it was publishing. The estimated postwar annual productive potential of the United States zone of Germany was 35,000 tons of newsprint, approximating 25 per cent of the German total, the Soviet zone being capable of producing 35 per cent, the British zone 30 per cent, and the French zone 10 per cent. However, due to the scarcity of coal and other manufacturing supplies, production in the American zone was unable to reach the maximum of its capacity. Soviet political and economic policy pursued on the Allied Control Council level made it virtually impossible to import paper and pulp from the Soviet zone, the largest single producer. Elsewhere in Europe, the position of paper stocks was critical. Importation of newsprint from the United States was ruled out because of the dollar-exchange problem, that is, because of the nonconvertibility of German Reichsmarks and occupation currency into dollars. Dollar credits likewise prohibited importation from neutral countries, such as Sweden, where supplies were abundant. The situation was such that only rapid over-all betterment of Germany's economic situation, Soviet co-operation with the Western Powers along the lines of the Anglo-American economic merger of their zones, and the treating of Germany as an economic unit as provided by the Potsdam Agreement, offered a way out from the impasse.

The official American Military Government newspaper *Die*

*Neue Zeitung* began publication on October 18, 1945, having continued publication after all other official newspapers had been replaced by the indigenous German press. It was distributed throughout the American zone of occupation in twice-weekly editions of approximately 1,500,000 copies.

Some Military Government officials believed—and this was especially true of Ambassador Robert Murphy, political adviser to the Military Governor—that *Die Neue Zeitung* should be published as a daily, with local editions for such key cities as Munich, Stuttgart and Berlin, and particularly in the latter city, where the shutting down of the official occupation newspaper there (the *Allgemeine Zeitung*) had been ordered by General Clay.[7] The prevailing opinion, however, was that the *Neue Zeitung* should not be identified with any particular locality, but should instead have a truly zone-wide character, and its size and frequency of publication not be inequitable with that allowed the German newspapers, so that it would not compete with them.

The life of the *Neue Zeitung*, as the life of many a new enterprise, was not a very smooth one. Numerous animadversions were directed against it, and on occasion it was charged with being "too German." Its first editor, Captain Hans Habe, thought it a mistake to give the Germans "merely an American newspaper" without compromising with German journalistic traditions. The *Zeitung* was what one might call an "elegant" newspaper, carrying art features and feuilletons, in appearance very appealing, owing, no doubt, to the fact that its editors collected the best of everything they could get, including ink, paper, and photographic and engraving equipment, and, in addition, it was printed in the modern and little-damaged printing plant of the Nazi Party's *Völkischer Beobachter*, in Munich. Chief criticism directed against the *Zeitung* during its first months of existence was that instead of being a vehicle for American views, and its material furnishing a picture of American life, it had gone in the opposite direction. Very little news

---

7. William Harlan Hale, "General Clay—On His Own," *Harper's Magazine*, CXCVII (December 1948), p. 88.

of the United States was included; less, in fact, than in many licensed newspapers. Its feature material was devoted to German culture, and material on American life and culture was conspicuous by its absence. Although presented in a highly skillful manner, the material was "for a German newspaper, not for an American newspaper for the German population."

In due course, the content of the *Neue Zeitung* began to conform to Military Government policy and to be shaped by official directives governing its publication. General McClure directed its editors to make their prime concern the communication to the German people of information about the United States and the American point of view on German and international affairs, "risking, if necessary, unpopularity at times." A high priority was to be given to news and feature material on the United States in order to overcome the long-standing provincial attitude of Germans toward our country. In common with the indigenous German press, the *Neue Zeitung* was to emphasize the need for the creation of a democratic Germany and institutions that would help achieve that goal. So as not to show flagrant favoritism and not to arouse possible hostility, the official organ was to be subject to the same material restrictions, such as the allocation of newsprint and printing supplies, as the licensed press. More and more, the *Neue Zeitung* was becoming the voice of Military Government, and after a year of publication was implementing directives under which it was published.[8]

As for the Germans, the *Zeitung* was well received by them. This was in part due to the general hunger for reading material among all classes of the population, and in part to its contents and excellent make-up. About half the adult population in the American zone read the paper and most of its readers preferred it to their own newspapers. Interestingly enough, a considerable number of its readers failed to realize that the *Zeitung* was an official Military Government organ. More middle-class and well-educated people read the paper than did

---

8. General McClure to Col. B. B. McMahon, July 17, 1946.

workingmen. The newspaper was liked for its variety of material and its considerable allotment of space to world news. It was favored by some for its high intellectual level and for the special features which were not found in the licensed newspapers. What criticism existed was directed against the absence of descriptions of ordinary people in American life and the way the average man lives, something in which most Germans displayed a keen interest.

Equally as important as the founding of newspapers was the development of technical competence and editorial confidence among licensed publishers and their employees. Since the Reich Ministry of Propaganda and Public Enlightenment had pressed nearly all newspapermen into its service through forced membership in the Federal Press Chamber, Military Government was at first forced to rely largely on inexperienced personnel to establish the new German press. Licensed newspapers were not infrequently amateurish and made errors in news evaluation and presentation. American press control officers had to guide and advise the new publishers on editorial problems and editorial discretion, as well as on business matters. Although the editors, as a rule, were full of the best intentions, the lack of proper printing plants, heat, newsprint, and of almost all other commodities, not to speak of food and housing, prevented the rapid emergence of a press less dull and dreary than the first issues of the licensed newspapers. They naturally compared unfavorably not only with American newspapers, but also with the average German provincial paper of pre-Hitler days.[9]

As far as individual newspapers went, the *Frankfurter Rundschau* was by far the most forceful and most outspoken. It concentrated mainly on news and editorials, and feature material was relegated to second place. Heidelberg's *Rhein-Neckar Zeitung*, on the other hand, devoted about half its space to features and less than ten per cent to world news. One of the liveliest among the first newspapers was the *Hessische Nach-*

9. Felix E. Hirsch, "The German Balance Sheet," *Current History*, XII (March 1947), p. 20.

*richten,* of Kassel. It struck a good balance between news and features, Military Government regulations were prominently printed, and the selection and treatment of news showed good editorial judgment and was of a high order. Munich's *Suddeutsche Zeitung* was a good newspaper and made a favorable impression. The *Frankenpost,* of Hof, on the other hand, was tabloid in format and sensational in content. Among the best newspapers in Bavaria was Augsburg's *Schwabische Landeszeitung,* which was well written and possessed a world outlook. In general, the public soon came to regard the licensed press as independent organs of German opinion and less as agents of the forces of occupation, an opinion which some people had held for a while. Only a minority offered articulate criticism, which came mostly from the well-to-do groups. Unlike readers from among workingmen, the better-to-do people missed news about plans affecting Germany's future, and they criticized their newspapers for it.

However, as time went on, the German press underwent considerable improvement. Newspapers were taking a more active part in the life of their communities and were increasingly able to solve their editorial and business problems themselves. The organization of associations of newspaper publishers in each *Land* of the American zone increased this self-reliance, and matters which formerly were dealt with by Military Government were taken up and settled by these associations.

The first step in encouraging newspaper competition, and thus preventing the creation of vested interests, was taken by Military Government in April 1946 when the *Neue Presse* was licensed in Frankfurt as a second newspaper to the *Rundschau.* It was the first paper to appear where a licensed German press was already in existence. Its political predilections were more to the "right" as compared with what was called the *Rundschau's* "left" leanings.[10]

The German press in the American zone, unlike that in the

---

10. ODIC/OMGUS, Press Release No. 30, April 13, 1946.

British and Soviet zones, was not a party press. Although it did not eschew political discussion, it was what might be called a "nonpolitical" press. Newspaper editors were selected exclusively from a journalistic point of view—but only after a careful investigation of their political backgrounds. While some critics adhered to the view that to deny political parties the right to publish newspapers is to deny the very basis of democratic political education, most Germans approved of a nonparty press and credited their newspapers with having remained impartial in discussing political problems. Only eight per cent of the readers early in 1947 favored a party press, 77 per cent were against it, and the rest were indifferent to the matter. Even some of the pre-Hitler party newspaper publishers favored the independent press, the most vocal demands for a party press coming from political leaders who were not concerned so much with creating a democratic press in Germany as with their own party's political fortunes. The underlying principle of our policy of a nonparty press was that such a press would prevent bitter political recrimination and thereby make easier the task of objectively reorientating German political thinking in accordance with American aims to see an impartial press prevail.

Subjects which were hardly touched by the newspapers in 1945 were a year later appearing in numerous articles and editorials—a sign of the wider interest publishers were taking in basic German and world problems. The apathy that pervaded the people, as well as public men who were relied upon by our government to take the lead in an ideological reorientation, was slowly but surely on the way to dissipation. This greater independence, however, had led some editors, on occasion, to write in contravention of press directives. The editor of *Suddeutsche Zeitung*, for example, on two separate occasions carried stories discrediting one of the occupying powers—namely, Soviet Russia—which was strictly against press regulations. And both of the Frankfurt newspapers—the *Rundschau* and the *Presse*—bitterly attacked the Military Government of Hesse for requisitioning buildings needed by the Army of occupation. Such attacks were, indeed, contrary to directives, which stipulated that no attacks on settled Military Government policy could be printed. In the one instance, the newspaper was ordered to reduce its editions from six to four pages for the period of one month; in the other, the editors were reprimanded and advised to keep strictly within the few limitations that still applied to them.

All in all, the German press could fairly be said to have been established as a free, democratic press. The growing differences between Russia and its satellite states on the one hand and the United States and Western Europe on the other were not hushed up. They were brought out objectively. The all-important question of German unity began constantly running through the press. Newspapers repeatedly emphasized it as a matter of great consequence to the German people. There were undertones of unmistakable disappointment in the failure of the great Powers to settle the German question. Germany had no future unless the zonal boundaries disappeared, editorialized one newspaper, and another saw utter economic collapse as a result. The *Wiesbadener Kurier* went so far as to state (July 16, 1946) that all progress made in the sphere of politics, *Länder* constitutions, and elections was well nigh useless so long as Germany remained partitioned.

There were numerous other instances of sober and unsensational treatment of news important to the future of Germany. The announcement by Secretary of State Byrnes in 1946 of the economic merger of the American and British zones of occupation was given factual treatment by most publishers. The predominant note struck by editorials was that the bipartite agreement did not exclude Soviet participation, whenever Soviet Russia decided to join, and meant to Western Germany much in practical potentialities for its economic reconstruction.

In Berlin, where the situation was unique in that each of the four occupying Powers licensed German newspapers in its own sector of the partitioned city, but permitted their sale throughout the former capital, of thirteen newspapers in circulation, the American-licensed *Der Tagesspiegel* was by far the most widely read, the British-licensed *Telegraf* running a close second. The French-licensed *Kurier* was third in preference, and the Soviet-licensed *Nacht Express*, fourth. As many as three fourths of Berlin's adult population read the *Tagesspiegel* regularly, preferring what was generally conceded to be its independent political stand to the one-sided stand of the press sponsored by Soviet Russia. The *Telegraf* was preferred to the others for the same reasons as the *Tagesspiegel*.

The German News Service (*DANA*) had its beginning in June 1945, when a small Military Government detachment arrived at Bad Nauheim to take over control of the 12th Army Group's press and radio facilities and the central publishing offices of the United States Army's German-language newspapers. Its beginnings were primitive. Correspondents were sent out to Berlin and Munich, and arrangements made with French and Soviet news agencies. Munich and Berlin were linked to Bad Nauheim by Morse telegraph; Frankfurt and Wiesbaden relied on a courier service. World news at first reached Germany from the Allied Press Service, in London, and later, when this wartime Anglo-American enterprise was terminated, from the United States Press Service in Luxembourg.

The name given the German news service was *Deutsche Allgemeine Nachrichten Agentur* or *DANA*, for short. On September 6 it began servicing newspapers and radio stations in the American zone with a complete file of world and German news as a consolidated agency. Operated directly by Military Government, technical operations were gradually entrusted to Germans until, after a twelve-month existence, *DANA* could be licensed as a nonprofit, co-operatively-owned enterprise, modelled organizationally somewhat along the lines of the Associated Press. It was owned and operated by the publishers of the newspapers in the American-occupied areas of Germany. Counting among its German journalistic staff in 1945 only three newspapermen, released from a prisoner of war camp at the behest of Military Government, a year later the news service was completely in German hands, free to conduct its own affairs, subject only to the few remaining restrictions applying to the indigenous press as a whole.

The German reader, to judge by surveys in cities where licensed newspapers were published, was satisfied that his paper, in the main, was sufficiently outspoken when occasion demanded. He felt that his paper had remained impartial in discussing political problems and felt that it had done a satisfactory job in helping the German people to gain a better understanding of the rest of the world, to improve understanding of, and friendship for, other nations, and to explain what was basically wrong in the philosophy and behavior of the National Socialist German Workers Party. In *DANA*, the German reader saw added evidence of the progressive movement leading from a controlled to an independent press.

# REVIVAL OF BOOK PUBLISHING
## AND PERIODICALS

## 4

AMERICAN MILITARY GOVERNMENT OFFICIALS, AS one authority aptly put it, were early confirmed in their belief that the book was a medium of great value in introducing rational, democratic ways of thinking in Germany.[1] They were fully aware that a good deal of literature would have to be brought in from the United States and Western Europe. On the other hand, these officials were equally aware that this could be only a small part of the much broader policy of the re-education of Germany by the Germans themselves. Finding politically "clean" and professionally qualified Germans, as in the newspaper field, was not the only problem. Distribution methods and retail outlets had to be developed, in a country that had become in every sense a four-headed hydra and had come practically to a complete economic and intellectual paralysis.

To fill the vacuum that existed between the time when German publishing activities were outlawed by Military Government Law 191 and when book publishing would again begin under Military Government control, about 35,000 copies each of 25 American books in German translation were supplied the population during the first months of the occupation. The supply of this type of literature was further increased by the establishment of a number of American Information Centers, which were combination libraries and reading rooms.[2]

---

1. H. Lehmann-Haupt, "The German Book Trade in 1945, Part II" *Publishers' Weekly*, CXLVIII (December 8, 1945), p. 2531.
2. *Report of the Military Governor*, p. 6; Paul Brooks, "Books Follow the Jeep," *Publishers' Weekly*, CXLVIII (December 8, 1945), p. 2528.

When Military Government took over control of the German book trade it was faced with an appalling situation. A very few only of the publishers had been permitted to continue in business by the German Government, and the bookstock on hand had been reduced to a small proportion of its peacetime capacity.[3] Military Government was, therefore, faced with no easy task in its efforts to get the German book publishing trade back on its feet. For example, when the first Information Control detachment entered Kassel, it found publishing plants and bookstores, like the rest of the city, almost completely destroyed. The one exception was a printer on the outskirts of the city whose presses were in good condition and who needed only electricity to get them running. Stuttgart, Germany's fifth-ranking city in publishing importance, was hardly in better condition. Ten publishing houses remained. Of more than one hundred bookstores only sixteen were in condition to do business at the war's end. The names and addresses of publishing concerns and bookstores had to be found by driving up one street and down the other, in the midst of rubble that made even the finding of streets an arduous task.

The first step Military Government took, after closing all book publishing and selling activities under Law 191, was to order the inventorying of books and the removal from bookshelves of all objectionable material. At the same time, bookstores whose owners were found politically unobjectionable were permitted to reopen. Growing out of practical necessity in the field, the practice was resorted to of placing bookdealers on their honor (where a thorough investigation of their political past was not possible in a short time) that they would not illegally sell books prohibited by Military Government. With but few exceptions the honor system worked. Violators were thenceforward barred from the business.

But many of the booksellers, especially in the big cities, had anticipated Military Government's moves and voluntarily segregated Nazi literature on their shelves. They had also

3. F. Reichmann, "The First Year of American Publications Control in Germany," *Publishers' Weekly*, CL (November 16, 1946), p. 2810.

( 45 )

started preparing lists of the books they felt would be on an Allied list of prohibited literature. The desire of what came to be called the "white" publishers, the men who had managed to a considerable degree to keep their publishing program free of Nazi doctrines, was, as Lehmann-Haupt states, to carry on as before.[4] It was on these publishers that Military Government began to rely for a revival of the German book publishing business.

Before a book publisher could engage in business he had to get a Military Government license, just as a newspaper editor had to. Licensing procedures were complicated and rigorous. The applicant had to file several questionnaires. After a thorough interview by a Military Government publications officer, the applicant, if approved, had to submit a publishing program for one year, worked out in specific titles. The program was then evaluated in terms of its worth to the development of democratic ideas and practices. The names of licensed publishers were then compiled by Military Government and published in the *Börsenblatt*, official organ of the book-trade, which was authorized to resume publication in Wiesbaden in October, 1945. Such publicity was intended to identify authorized publishers to whom authors could submit their manuscripts and from whom dealers could order stock. It was not the author, then, but the publisher, who was held responsible for bringing out the type of literature desired by the American Government, and it was he who was held liable in case of a breach of Military Government directives and regulations. New books were scrutinized by publications control officers, and violators prosecuted. In minor and first cases, warning was given and the book confiscated. More severe punishment consisted of suspension or revocation of the publisher's license and prosecution before a Military Government court.

The size of every edition was limited to 5,000 copies. An edition of more than that number had to be applied for—giving reasons why a larger edition should be permitted—and was

---

4. Lehmann-Haupt, *loc. cit.*, p. 2532.

approved only when it could be established that the content of the book was of such a nature that it would make an exceptional contribution to the re-education of the German people and that the larger edition was needed to meet minimum costs of production. The acute paper shortage, as we have shown before, was the main reason for this restrictive policy. As an early, and, it would seem, feeble attempt partially to overcome the paper shortage (and partially as a means of destroying Nazi literature without resorting to book burning) Military Government decided to delegate to German civil agencies the task of segregating and arranging for pulping publications which it had outlawed. The shortage of raw materials and production facilities was another reason for the limited editions. Paper mills were often located in one zone, fuel to run them in another. In Berlin, many of the printing facilities were located in one occupation sector, publishers and booksellers in all four, and the absence of adequate economic intercourse between the Soviet sector of the city and those occupied by the Western Powers prevented a more rapid revival of book publishing. Since the book trade could not be re-established on a nationwide or interzonal scale, the United States re-established the *Börsenverein*, the old German book-trade association, on a zone-wide basis, with headquarters in Wiesbaden. The *Verein* provided a central machinery for fair trade practices, the control of prices, and the dissemination of regulations issued by the occupation authorities.

American government policy governing the licensing of publishers differed from that of the other occupying Powers. Essentially, our procedure emphasized the selection of anti-Nazis, to conform to the more rigorous denazification policy in effect in our zone; the British placed about equal stress on the applicant's political record and his ability to produce desirable publications; the Soviets stressed production only, permitting almost any applicant to engage in the publishing business if his books and magazines passed the censor before they were released for circulation. The consequence of this difference in policy was that the other Powers were ahead in point of production, but in our zone, it was believed, the policy followed would lay a more durable foundation for a democratically dependable book publishing enterprise, that could be trusted to continue in its task of ideological reorientation even after Military Government controls were relaxed or entirely removed.

The first license to publish books in the American zone was granted in July 1945 to a publisher named Hermann Meister, of Heidelberg, whose program consisted of works of general interest, prominent among which was a reprint of the *Autobiography of Benjamin Franklin.* In Bavaria, four publishers of religious books were licensed to publish catechisms, hymn books, and other religious literature. Soon followed licensing in Berlin, where the owners of the firm Gebr. Mann were authorized to publish works on art and archaeology. A Protestant minister, Ernst Rhein, was granted permission to publish a monthly official church bulletin for the Protestant churches of Zehlendorf. By the end of 1945 some 76 publishers had been licensed, their publishing programs ranging from general literature and social science to religious and technical subjects. Thirty titles had been published by the end of 1945, including several novels. Karl Barth's *Toward the Rehabilitation of the German Character,* comprising a series of theologio-philosophical essays, bore the distinction of being the first post-war book published under American Military Government. Public lectures on modern education and a number of medical works were also among the books published.

The number of licensed publishers increased rapidly to some 250 by late 1946. The number of titles, including pamphlets, had increased to over one thousand.[5] Among the important new books were such titles as *The Leader and the Misled* by Hans Windisch, *The Rebirth of the German Spirit* by Karl Barth, and *The Idea of a University* by Karl Jaspers.

On the whole, early postwar German authorship was poor. Military Government was therefore forced to turn to the United States for good books, and attempts were made to obtain translation rights of American works. Great efforts were exerted in

---

5. *Report of the Military Governor,* op. cit., p. 6.

that direction since there was a ready market in Germany for American books, but, on the whole, these efforts were not very successful.

One major difficulty stood in the way of this program: getting American authors to sell their German translation rights to German publishers at a flat rate of $250, which the United States Government offered them, when they could sell these same rights to Swiss publishers, who paid considerably more. The government, of course, took the attitude that American writers had a stake in the re-education of the German people and should therefore disregard the higher pecuniary rewards offered by Swiss publishers. Besides, the trouble was that when American rights *were* sold to the Swiss, the American zone of Germany could not import these books. The reason for this was that Swiss publishers would not accept payment in German Reichsmarks and Military Government did not possess American dollars for that purpose. Yet, it was well known that American authors did not have to sell *all* their German rights to the Swiss—they could have reserved their rights for Germany to the United States Government. The plain truth of the matter is that some writers would have nothing to do with the Germans, clinging to the theory that they were *all* guilty—of everything and anything—and, therefore, incorrigible. Some American authors, however, disregarding the financial aspects of the case, did sell the German rights to their books to the government for publication in Germany. Notable among them were: Van Wyck Brooks, Carl Sandburg, Ernest Hemingway, William Maxwell, and Irving Stone.

Once they were purchased by the United States Government, translation rights were assigned to Military Government in Germany, which then selected the publishers and assured compliance with the terms of the original contract. The government, as we have stated, paid the flat sum of $250 for the rights to each title. All receipts over $250, however, went into blocked accounts in Reichsmarks to the benefit of the American copyright owners. When a German publisher agreed to print an American book, a contract, containing the terms made by the government with the original copyright owner, was drawn up by which the publisher had to abide. One of the reasons why some American authors were reluctant to sell their rights for publication in Germany was their inability to draw on the accounts that Military Government established and held in trust for them. Neither the Reichsmark, the regular German currency, nor the occupation mark, the supplementary currency introduced by the Allies, was convertible into dollars.

As for periodicals, quite a variety began to appear not long after the cessation of hostilities. The first to appear was a periodical called *Die Wandlung*, a literary and scholarly publication produced in Heidelberg. It was followed by periodicals such as *Der Bogen*, of Wiesbaden; *Der Standpunkt*, of Stuttgart; *Sie*, a women's magazine, of Berlin; and *Ulenspiegel*, a periodical of satire modeled along the lines of the old *Simplicissimus*, also of Berlin. In rapid succession there appeared *Die Lucke*, a religio-cultural periodical, published in Heidelberg; *Der Pinguin*, a youth magazine, published in Stuttgart; and *Der Horizont*, another youth magazine, in Berlin. The two youth magazines had become so popular that by the summer of 1946, Military Government authorized the circulation of the one to be increased from 50,000 to 200,000 copies and of the other from 125,000 to 250,000 copies.

Professional technical periodicals also made their appearance, such as a farm journal, a theatrical magazine, and one of radio news and comment. A small Marxist journal, *Das Neue Wort*, appeared in Stuttgart. By late 1946, a total of some 130 periodicals was thus in circulation in the American occupation areas of Germany.

As in the case of the official Military Government newspaper *Die Neue Zeitung*, several official periodicals were published for the German people. They were the *Amerikanische Rundschau, Heute*, and *Neue Auslese*. The first two were American Military Government organs and the third was an Anglo-American one.

Modeled somewhat after *Harper's Magazine*, the *Amerikanische Rundschau* went on sale in August 1945, catering to the intellectual reader. It carried American authors only, presenting trends in American cultural life. What readers liked best were the articles on political and economic questions and science, some expressing surprise that the United States had something to offer besides businessmen. What appears to have been wanting in sufficient measure, however, was discussion of American social life, a subject that interested many Germans.

*Heute* was an illustrated magazine, in format slightly smaller than *Life*, but very much like it in its make-up. It was directed to the general reading public and made its appeal mainly to the moderately informed reader. In its approach, *Heute* was neither narrowly intellectual and specialist nor sensationally journalistic, and as an official publication of Military Government its editorial policy eschewed purely German problems, German writers, or German culture.[6]

The history of *Heute* is an interesting one. It first appeared in September 1945, the first issue proving rather disappointing to many of its readers. It stressed war themes too much, and the theme of collective guilt, of which most Germans were by then tired. The whole tone was accusatory and attempted to direct people's attention to the devastation and suffering Germany had brought on. These themes had, of course, been in keeping with the so-called "austerity" policy under which the Office of War Information was then functioning, chief proponents of which were William Harlan Hale and George Backer.[7] In this spirit, the first and second issues were published in London in July and August 1945, and shipped to Germany to be sold in September and October, respectively. By that time the "collective guilt" idea had completely failed of acceptance by the German people. Pro-democratic people of all shades resented the continued harping on that theme, and the mission of the occupation of reorientating German thinking was not being helped thereby a single iota. No wonder that *Heute* at first had little

6. OMGUS, *Military Government Information Bulletin*, No. 71 (December 9, 1946), pp. 11-12.
7. Alfred V. Boerner, Deputy Chief of Publications Section, ODIC, OMGUS, to the author, March 13, 1946.

appeal. But with the change of policy that began to take place toward the end of the year, when the "collective guilt" idea was abandoned and a differentiation made between those who were actively guilty of starting the war and those who were mere passive bystanders, considerable improvement was made in the contents of the magazine. The themes in successive issues began to take on a brighter tone. They had a message to deliver—one that looked to the future and its many problems. Publication was moved from London to Munich, thereby bringing editorial policy in closer contact with conditions in Germany and more in line with the broader aspects of Military Government aims.

*Neue Auslese* was a joint British-American periodical. In appearance and content it was very much like *Reader's Digest*. It presented material chosen widely from current American magazines, including articles, short stories and poetry, but carrying contributions also by British, French, and Russian writers. Its avowed purpose was to bring to the German reader the best in European literary creation and to help overcome his years of intellectual isolation from the best of non-German literature.

With the revival of the publication of books and periodicals and with the controls and guidance exercised by Military Government, another foundation, it was hoped, had been laid for a reorientation of German thinking along democratic paths.

# THE REHABILITATION
# OF GERMAN RADIO

## 5

THE RADIO NETWORK IN GERMANY WAS COMPRISED of three separate autonomous systems—American, British, and Russian. It was controlled by the respective occupying Powers.

In the American-occupied areas, the network, with its key station at Luxembourg, was operated by military and Office of War Information civilian personnel, with German civilians in certain technical and writing positions. It consisted at first of Radio Munich, the first to go on the air, May 12; Radio Frankfurt, which began broadcasting on June 2; followed by Radio Stuttgart, which opened on June 3. To these were later added Radio Bremen, and the *Drahtfunk*, a wired means of radio reception operating in the American sector of Berlin.

Like newspapers and books, radio was employed by Military Government to promote the program of re-education. The method used was to report news factually, by divorcing it from opinion. A fair amount of radio time was allotted to material, showing how the political systems in democratic countries work. Round-table discussions were put on the air. As the Germans were granted greater responsibility in the preparation of programs—gradually replacing Military Government personnel—freedom of expression was allowed them within the scope of official directives, and equal time allocated to all political parties, particularly at election time. Cultural programs and music characteristic of other countries were regularly presented in an attempt to integrate some non-German cultural influences into the daily life of the country. In addition, the allocation of radio time was balanced in a way so as not to destroy the fundamental value of the medium, namely entertainment.

It was not merely with thinking up and preparing the right programs that American authorities were faced. First and foremost, they had the problem on their hands of rebuilding the studios and transmitters. Most of them had been shattered by the war well nigh beyond recognition.

As long as Radio Luxembourg, one of Europe's most powerful transmitters, continued to serve as the key station for the American network, it kept on feeding programs to the other more or less makeshift stations in occupied territory. However, when the station was returned to the government of Luxembourg in November 1945, Radio Frankfurt assumed control of American network operations—between Frankfurt, Stuttgart, and Munich. This new network was linked by land lines.

Radio Munich, the first on German soil to begin broadcasting to the German people, was found by American troops in a semi-destroyed condition. Although the transmitter was comparatively intact, power cables leading to it and the building housing the studios were badly damaged. The first broadcast, made on May 10, 1945, was therefore a makeshift affair, American radio specialists all the while working on repairs and the hiring of German technical personnel and announcers. From a beginning of mere news relays from Luxembourg and the broadcasting of Military Government announcements, at the end of the first thirty days, broadcast time had increased to ten and one-half hours daily.

Gradually, as rehabilitation proceeded, broadcasting time increased, and programs, instead of originating in Luxembourg, were planned and prepared in Munich itself. Local and world news was prominently featured; special programs for the farmer were put on; there also were programs for youth, women, and displaced persons, as well as discussions of public affairs.

The career of Radio Frankfurt began on June 2, 1945 as a 1 kw. transmitter, which was some weeks later increased to 20 kw., when a German transmitter was installed. This station distinguished itself for the first postwar broadcast by a German from Germany to the people of the United States, the occasion being a short-wave speech by the mayor of Frankfurt to the *Herald-Tribune* Forum in New York.

Radio Stuttgart, the last of the three larger stations to go on the air, was a veritable shambles when first taken over by Military Government. For a good many weeks the main task consisted of clearing away debris and repairing physical plant, carried on amidst shortages of every kind. It began its broadcasts with a program of 28 hours weekly, gradually expanding it as facilities and technical and writing personnel improved.

In Berlin, the rehabilitation of radio centered around Radio Berlin and the *Drahtfunk*. The problem of Radio Berlin involved considerable, but fruitless, wrangling with Russia in the Allied Control Council and in the Kommandatura, since the station's studios were located in the British sector of the city, and by right subject to British Military Government control, and the transmitters in the French sector, and by the same right subject to French Military Government control. But the Russians, who had occupied the transmitter site as well as the studios from the very day Berlin fell to them, had made Radio Berlin—a very powerful station—their own, refusing to let the other occupying Powers have a voice in its management. This was, of course, illegal, since all physical plant in any one sector of the city automatically came, like property in a zone of occupation in the rest of Germany, under the sole control of the particular Power occupying that sector.

More than once did the United States Military Government, supported by its British and French counterparts, recommend that Radio Berlin, located as it was in a quadripartite city, be operated on a quadripartite basis, with equal time allotted to all occupying Powers. So modest, in fact, were the American proposals that it is difficult to believe that they were ever rejected by the Russians. The proposals were never acted upon. They called for one hour each day to be allotted to each of the occupying Powers to broadcast Military Government announcements (the station all the time remaining under Soviet administrative control) and local entertainment programs to be under the control of a quadripartite committee. This, in American opinion, was all that could be hoped for. But it soon turned out that hopes had been running too high.

Numerous attempts to negotiate with the Russians revealed that they interpreted the one-hour-per-day proposal as meaning a total of one hour of radio time for the Americans, British, and French combined. And after involving the Western nations in polemics extending over many months, they began to develop the theme that, in any case, Radio Berlin was the only radio outlet in the Russian zone of occupation and therefore they had decided to control it unilaterally. The fact that the city of Berlin was in nowise a part of any zone of occupation carried no weight with the Russians. Furthermore, Radio Leipzig, in the Russian zone of Germany went on the air on September 13 and the Russians were even then preparing Radio Magdeburg and Radio Dresden for broadcasting.

Needless to say, this was an entirely unsatisfactory situation to the three Western Powers. And it was in this situation that American Military Government decided to activate the *Drahtfunk*, a radio system transmitting programs over wires, somewhat in the manner of a telephone. Special arrangements had to be made to connect an ordinary radio set to the *Drahtfunk*. During the war the Germans used it to make special local broadcasts they did not want Allied monitors to pick up. To get the *Drahtfunk* functioning it was at first necessary to install a broadcast line from Frankfurt to Berlin, so that programs originating at Radio Frankfurt and the other stations in the American zone could be relayed to Berlin.

Connected to a relatively small proportion of Berlin's radio sets (13 per cent), the *Drahtfunk* began to broadcast in February 1946, and although many of its listeners liked the impartial news and commentary they were getting, that in no way made up for the inadequacy of its entertainment programs as compared with those of Radio Berlin. True enough, there was widespread dissatisfaction in the city with the Soviet-controlled station, because of its undisguised political onesidedness and hostility to anyone and anything that did not support Soviet policies, but with its entertainment offerings few had any quarrels. Thus, in Berlin, the influence of the American educational and cultural programs was extremely limited and we were in no position to compete with the Russians who spared neither talent nor money to advance their objectives.

A saving feature in this radio "war," if one may call it that, was the broadcasts from the British zone of Germany, which enjoyed considerable popularity among those with sets capable of receiving stations from that zone. In view of this fact, British Military Government erected a special transmitter in its sector of Berlin over which these broadcasts were relayed; and this in some ways solved the problem of keeping Berliners informed of the Western points of view on German and international affairs.

The British action was followed up by our government in the autumn of 1946 with the establishment of a new station called Radio Station in the American Sector, or RIAS, for short. It was connected to the *Drahtfunk* and transmitted the programs which the latter received from the American zone of Germany. Thus was not only all of greater Berlin covered, but even a fairly wide area around the city in Soviet-occupied Germany.[1]

To meet our needs in the Bremen enclave, which is separated from the American zone by the British zone of occupation, Radio Bremen was founded in October 1945, first as a mobile transmitter and some weeks later as a permanent station.

From the very outset, large numbers of radio listeners were, in the main, pleased with the programs broadcast by the American network. Radio Frankfurt dominated the field in the early days, though some objection was raised to the number of foreign language programs which were directed at displaced persons. In Bavaria, Radio Munich grew in popularity. On the whole, light operetta, symphonic, and operatic music

---

1. OMGUS, War Department, September 25, 1946.

were the favored forms of entertainment. A good many of the young people responded favorably to the "Jazz Hours."

Good popular American music was receiving an ever wider audience in Germany. A program called "The Ten of the Week" (similar to the "Hit Parade") was a favorite, since the ten most popular American songs it featured were chosen on the basis of a listeners' poll. A German version of "Information Please" was another of the more successful programs. A number of educational programs began finding their way over the radio stations working in close co-operation with school authorities. In this field, Radio Stuttgart led the way, broadcasting the first school program in December 1945, followed by Radio Frankfurt and RIAS.[2]

Radio broadcasting and the management of radio stations were begun, as we have already had occasion to point out, as out-and-out Military Government undertakings. However, as a part of General Clay's program of turning all propaganda and culture media over to the Germans as soon as possible, steps were taken to set the stations up as publicly owned German corporations, with American officials exercising only a most general policy supervision. In this process of "turning over," at first, American technical personnel was withdrawn, followed by supervisory and policy-making staffs. For broad guidance of the radio station under our control, an American Network Control Office was organized to co-ordinate the implementation of policy by the various stations and to maintain postbroadcast scrutiny. In addition, each *Land* government had agreed to establish a public corporation in its area. Privately-owned commercial stations, on American lines, though not prohibited by Military Government law, were not even considered by the German state governments, since radio broadcasting had traditionally been state-owned in Germany and was financed by public funds collected as fees on radio receivers. The charters that were prepared for these public corporations, providing

---

2. Harry A. Jacobs, "Education by Radio," *Military Government Information Bulletin*, No. 151, (December 28, 1948), p. 9 ff.

against the possibility of political interference in broadcasting, ensured radio's representing all organized elements of the population, such as educational institutions, trade unions, religious federations, and the like, and legally safeguarded the carrying out of the fundamental aims of developing a democratic Germany.

# THE MOTION PICTURE
# IN THE SCHEME OF THINGS

## 6

FROM THE VERY BEGINNING OF THE OCCUPATION ALL German-made motion pictures were impounded and the famous Bavaria *Filmkunst* studios requisitioned. The showing of films remained banned under Military Government Law No. 191 until July 30, 1945, when 16 theaters opened in our zone of occupation and four in our sector of Berlin. The films shown were the Anglo-American newsreel *Welt im Film* and the American documentaries *Toscanini* and *TVA*.

More theaters, however, were soon opened, numbering 50 in mid-September and showing full-length Hollywood features subtitled in German. This progress was not as rapid as was hoped for. Although the destruction done in Germany during the war took its toll from public and residential buildings as well as from industrial plants, the real difficulty in getting more motion picture houses opened lay in the short supply of films. Not only did Military Government not have enough titles at its disposal, but it lacked, as well, a sufficient number of copies of each title to go around to all the theaters that were in good enough condition to open for business. There were, all in all, available only some 30 feature titles in the immediate posthostilities months, 15 commercial shorts, and about 25 documentaries (all varying from five to six copies each), sufficient to service only something like 150 motion picture theaters, whereas there were actually three times that number found capable of opening for business in Bavaria alone.

This seemingly easy problem might have been solved, but

for one very important factor—the inability of the American motion picture industry to co-operate along policy lines laid down by the United States Government for the occupation of Germany. True, the Bavarian studios, which American troops had captured intact, were capable of processing about 1,500,000 feet of positive film per week, but the demands the motion picture companies were making on the United States Government in return for permission to print more copies of their films were so inconsistent with occupation policy that they failed to reach a mutually satisfactory agreement. The industry's conditions did not fall far short of virtual ownership of the studios and control of the film market in Germany.

That more motion picture theaters had to be opened was scarcely questioned by anyone in Germany, nor that the German people had to be provided with some form of normal diversion. There seemed only two ways out of the impasse, and even then they only partially overcame the acute film shortage. One way was to release several Hollywood features which had previously, at the request of the film industry that there be equal participation of the leading companies in the German market, been withheld. In other words, in order that no more films of one company than that of another would be shown, a partially artificial shortage had been created. The second way out was by releasing some German films that had, in the meantime, been impounded and censored. Thus the first German films, approved for their "harmlessness," were for the first time released by Military Government in December, 1945. It is worth noting, however, that the motion picture industry did not take very kindly to this procedure, hoping to establish as near an exclusive position in Germany as it could.

In this contest between supply and demand—the film industry and Military Government—the bipartite Anglo-American newsreel *Welt im Film* became a factor of some significance. Production of the reel was increased and moved from England to the Bavaria studios. Suggestions from some quarters that the newsreel be reduced in scope was promptly turned down, both by American Military Government in Germany and the Political Intelligence Division of the British Foreign Office—partner in the enterprise.

Another aspect of the situation—and an important reason why Hollywood was not allowed a free hand in Germany—was the need of getting the German motion picture industry started again as a *German* business enterprise, not as an American one. The view of our government was that there was to be no economic exclusivism in our occupation of Germany. The course was therefore adopted of giving every encouragement to German motion picture producers with "clean"—that is, non-Nazi—political records to apply to Military Government for permission to organize film production.

Just as the introduction into Germany of the best of American books depended on the degree of co-operation of their authors, the introduction of the best in the American film depended on the co-operation of the motion picture industry. The degree of this co-operation was of utmost importance to our government, since the producing companies were owners of their pictures and merely sold—or rented—them for exhibition under stipulated conditions. It was the *conditions* that formed the stumbling block to a successful quantitative, at least, motion picture program in Germany, not to mention the fact that in terms of quality, for purposes of re-educating a defeated nation, Hollywood was not too rich a source to draw on.

Since Hollywood controlled the film market, Hollywood films it had to be. But from the very beginning, the industry, through its European representatives in Paris and on the staff of Military Government in Germany as distribution experts, made serious efforts to convince occupation authorities that it be allowed to establish what would in effect have amounted to a monopoly of not only motion picture distribution, but of production and the ownership of theaters as well. The industry even interposed objections to the showing of German films for fear of competition. The industry was induced to oppose the showing of German films by a desire to have its own control of the market in Germany.

But this was not all. The motion picture companies were

also interested in obtaining the use of the Bavarian *Filmkunst* studios for the production of pictures, and with their extensive resources had hoped to get in on the ground floor, so to speak. This, of course, was contrary to the objectives which the United States Government had mapped out for the German motion picture industry. Government policy, as stated by General McClure, was to encourage and give material aid to approved German film producers as part of the over-all policy of stimulating indigenous cultural services and of turning them over to German ownership, to be kept under Military Government guidance for as long as conditions might dictate. Under this policy, it was scarcely deemed advisable to make German production facilities available to American firms, especially when German producers were already preparing to resume production on their own. In this connection, it had become the policy of Military Government to see that the re-established German film industry separated the production end of the business from distribution. This separation of distribution from production was motivated by a desire to shy away from establishing exclusive enterprise and to allow free competition.

As time went by, the number of American films shown in Germany slowly increased, and more theaters were gradually opened. Yet it can be said that at no time were there enough films to meet requirements. There existed also the problem of showing the *proper type* of film, for one that was very successful with Americans could easily prove a failure with German audiences. Considerable discrimination had to be exercised, but even then the gap between what was desirable and what was available could never quite be bridged. In consequence, Hollywood repeatedly used its controlling position to force concessions from the government. For the latter found itself in a helpless, as well as hopeless, position. It did have available a number of shorts produced during the war by the Office of War Information, but no sustained film program could be carried out on those. The government was virtually faced with a situation of "either . . . or . . . "

One important factor that contributed to the motion picture

industry's unwillingness to increase sufficiently its supply of films to Germany was the question of dollars. As already explained in our discussion of book publishing, the film companies could not get the money they earned in Germany out of that country, since German currency was not convertible into dollars. An additional factor that held back our program was that the industry wanted only the major eight or ten companies to export to Germany. This ran straight into strong opposition from Military Government, which wanted to include independent producers in order to obtain the best product. Military Government was little interested in who produced a given film so long as, in its judgment, it was a good one.

Attempts to get the motion picture industry to agree to conditions that would not compromise occupation objectives in Germany failed. When General McClure returned to Germany in December 1945 from a series of conferences with leaders of the film industry in the United States, he could report little save that the industry had shown a desire to utilize the military occupation to establish an exclusive position for American films and American distribution machinery. The position our government took, as the General explained, was that we had only a moral obligation to aid the film companies and then only if they agreed to the policies and objectives in force in Germany. It amounted to saying, in effect, that "whoever knows what the Germans need and what our government wants to teach them will be allowed to do business in Germany."[1] A situation like that could not, however, last very long. It became increasingly doubtful in 1946 that the motion picture industry would withdraw from its position and increasingly more evident that concessions on the part of the government would have to be made, especially when the possibility had developed by mid-summer that the industry might ultimately refuse to make films available unless an acceptable proposal for their reimbursement of dollar expenditures was worked out. The income which the film companies derived from the exhibition of their films could only be

1. The author's notes, taken at a staff meeting of the Information Control Division, USFET, in Bad Homburg, December 11, 1945.

in the form of blocked accounts, held to their credit by Military Government until such time as Reichsmarks could be converted into dollars and taken out of the country. There was little or nothing, however, to prevent the use of German money within Germany. And it was in this respect, it would appear, that the film companies held a strong position. They suggested the employment of Reichsmarks for the outright acquisition of German motion picture theaters, for the production by them in German studios of newsreels for release both in Germany and other countries, and for the purchase of German raw stock to make positives of pictures to be shown in Germany as well as outside it. The government, on the other hand, was opposed to such economic penetration, particularly to the acquisition of theaters and other real estate, for it would seriously have limited the participation of the Germans in the rebuilding of their country. The question was even mooted in some government quarters of the total substitution of German films for American. But this had to be given up as unworkable.

The situation was complex. Military Government could flatly have turned down the motion picture industry's conditions. Then again, it could not, unless it wished to defeat its own purpose.

The solution was a compromise—the old and tried method of give and take. At American Military Government headquarters in Berlin, opinion ran that, though contrary to government policy, limited American financial participation in the German motion picture industry would have to be tolerated. Furthermore, in view of the policies developed by the other two Western Powers in their zones, France allowing a German company, in which French film distibutors were heavily interested, to act as the sole distribution agency, and Great Britain organizing a British-controlled firm, operating a distribution agency and a chain of cinemas, the American position was considered somewhat singular. Still another factor that made for compromise—on the part of the United States Government, that is—was the plans on the part of German *Land* governments of socialization. What our government wanted to see was a private, nonmonopolistic motion picture industry; an industry based, as much as possible, on laissez faire principles. The position was taken that the motion picture companies be allowed to engage in the production and distribution of pictures in the American zone of Germany but not in their exhibition. Beyond permitting a strictly limited number of movie houses to be directly connected with the producing companies as first-run cinemas, the participation of American capital through the acquisition of theaters was ruled out. It was, in addition, considered unwise to permit private firms to compete with the official Anglo-American newsreel *Welt im Film*. And lastly, the industry's proposal to use German raw stock for the production of newsreels for its export trade was disapproved on the ground that according to the Potsdam Agreement export from Germany could not be considered unless internal German needs had been met first.

The standards set for films to be shown in Germany, within limits made possible by the available supply, were high. From among the number made available by the film companies, only the best were selected. Quality was what Military Government stressed.

Representative of American films shown were: *Pride and Prejudice, Dr. Ehrlich's Magic Bullet, The Gold Rush, Abraham Lincoln in Illinois, Tom, Dick, and Harry, Here Comes Mr. Jordan, Madame Curie, Young Tom Edison, It Happened Tomorrow*, and the like. Also documentaries such as *Toscanini, TVA, Pipeline, The Cowboy, Steel Town, The Jeep, Building of Boys*, and *Democracy in Action*. There were, besides, some British, French, and Russian films shown based on a quadripartite exchange agreement, as well as German pictures.

The reactions of German audiences to American films were mixed. Very popular was the newsreel *Welt im film*, audiences not infrequently going to the movies just to see news. Documentaries, too, enjoyed considerable favor.

Of Hollywood features, most popular were light comedies. Films like *You Were Never Lovelier, The Gold Rush, It Started With Eve*, and *Seven Sweethearts* had the biggest box-office attraction. Historical and biographical films, such as *Abraham Lincoln in Illinois* and *Madame Curie*, were in the next best-liked group. *Going My Way* proved extremely successful, particularly in Bavaria, with its large Catholic population, where it was considered an ideal type of film. War films were received with widespread disapproval and even hostility, and in most instances their release had either to be curtailed or withdrawn altogether after a few showings. Pictures like *Action in the North Atlantic*, *Corvette K-225*, and *The Navy Comes Through*, shown during the first months of the occupation in order to impress the Germans with Allied strength and to convince them of their own war guilt, had, before long, to be withdrawn.

What Germans wanted to see most were films dealing with the lives of average American families. The few dealing with the subject that were shown were well received. Films that were received with indifference and had the lowest box-office attraction were fantasy films, such as *Here Comes Mr. Jordan*, *All That Money Can Buy*, and *Flesh and Fantasy*. The imaginative situations in these and similar films were apparently alien to the German cinema-goer's mind.

Taken as a whole, it soon became apparent that the Hollywood film was not held in high regard by most Germans. Although, to some extent, this could be attributed to the language difficulties and the use of subtitles, the low opinion of its worth was due to the very quality of film generally produced in Hollywood. To this should be added the fact that certain types of film, liked in the United States, were not at all liked in Germany. The country's different cultural and entertainment standards, its different traditions, and its very different sense of humor and of tragedy accounted for a good measure of dissatisfaction with the Hollywood product. All this, in spite of the fact that Military Government selected for showing in Germany qualitatively only the best that money could buy.

It was a puzzling situation, to say the least. Fundamentally, we were in Germany for the purpose of undoing the propaganda work of the Nazi regime and of redirecting German culture along traditional Western patterns. Could the Hollywood film, from the point of view of its educational value, serve the purpose? Apparently, the Germans' answer was that it could not. And for the very good reason, as one man interested in this subject said,[2] that work of a higher standard will have to be done by Hollywood if that center is not to continue to be more of an international liability than an asset. The trouble with the Hollywood film, from the point of view of its educational value, is that it distorts the picture of American life. Much too often it is about glamorous love, not often enough a basic American—or universal—historical, educational, or just plain human theme. The industry, too steeped in its own conception of "the better side of life," handicapped rather than aided our mission in Germany.

---

2. A. L. Mander, *Foundations of Modern World Society*, Stanford, Califorornia, 1947, p. 541.

# RENAISSANCE IN THE THEATER, OPERA AND MUSIC

## 7

THAT THE THEATER AND MUSIC HAVE A GREAT TRADI-
tion in Germany, is well known to many. One authority on
German culture recently went so far as to state that its drama
and music stand for something that can almost be called a
religion in itself. Whereas in the United States and Great
Britain they are classed as "entertainment," in Germany these
two arts have been for two centuries or more what the Germans
call a *mythos*.[1]

The close of the war found all theatrical and musical life
at a complete standstill. Like everything else, the classical media
in which the noble in the spirit of mankind has been un-
folded most eloquently had been left by the war in a state of
almost complete annihilation. Practically the whole of life and
culture had to be rebuilt, and many Germans turned to the
theater and music as an escape from the sordidness of life. To
many, as after the First World War, the arts "assumed a role of
first importance in the struggle . . . for a new direction to their
existence."[2] Not unlike other peoples, the Germans knew that
in these arts the noble and the ignoble, the eminent and the
base, the illustrious and the sordid stand counterpoised—to be
used by men of artful politics to foster rabid emotional passion
or by magnanimous men of humanism to foster virtue and
spiritual sublimity. Those who had not by Nazi ideology been

---

1. Edward J. Dent, "Music and Drama in Germany," *The Contemporary
   Review*, CLXX (October 1946), p. 216.
2. Otto Manthey-Zorn, *Germany in Travail*, Boston, 1922, p. 62.

brutalized beyond redemption sought in the classical drama and in music a refuge and a hope. And it was the special task of the occupation, in the midst of indescribable (one had to see it to believe it) destruction and moral corruption to utilize the theater and music as a great spiritual force for the restoring of Germany to a healthy state of mind. Military Government, therefore, carefully set out to cultivate it. It met with considerable success.

As in the other cultural media, the Germans were left to organize their own dramatic and musical activities, though under Military Government's political supervision. The political background of every German theatrical producer, director, actor, variety performer, and ballet dancer was carefully scrutinized and all activities, whether in the serious drama or the variety pun, watched for any sort of prohibited political tendency.

But not so at first. Amid the somewhat confusing trends of troop redeployment—the bane of the occupation in the early days, the lack of understanding on the part of many troop commanders of the function of Military Government, and the friction between the strictly military commands and Military Government units over their relationship to one another, more than one German performer on the Military Government "black list" managed to earn a living. Many a troop unit special service officer, anxious to employ whatever talent was at hand to entertain his troops, who were "sweating out" that long trip home, paid little heed to Military Government directives. More often than not he had not even heard of them. Theaters, opera houses, and concert halls that had not been destroyed beyond repair by military operations were used as Red Cross clubs and a variety of other purposes without regard to the Germans' needs. There was lacking also the political awareness that from the very moment hostilities ceased on the night of May 8, 1945 the problem in Germany was first and foremost a Military Government problem, that is, the problem of the relationship of the United States Government, through its armed forces, to the German people.

The long efforts of Information Control staffs of Military Government to get the imposing Wiesbaden opera house in service for the revival of German cultural life, instead of for the exclusive use of troops, is an example of the case in point. In Stuttgart, the *Staatstheater* was requisitioned for troops and only grudgingly shared with the German population on days when it was not used for troops entertainment. Incidents were numerous in which Germans of dubious political reputation performed before military organizations. In Nürnberg, a whole local operatic company, containing a number of Nazi party members, was employed by a tank destroyer battalion, and the divine music of the immortal Beethoven flowed from the fingers of Walter Gieseking, renowned and superb artist, but equally renowned "cultural" agent abroad of the Ministry of Propaganda and Public Enlightenment of the Third German Reich.

A lack of knowledge of Military Government policy in the spheres of theater and music, and some carelessness and indifference, were the crosscurrents Military Government staffs had to overcome in more than one locality before they could devote their full time to the prime task of encouraging a renaissance in the theater and in music. However, with the passing months, affairs took on a semblance of order, and clarity emerged. Military Government laws and regulations began to be strictly enforced, and the now familiar machinery of denazification, investigation, and licensing began to function smoothly. Thus the first licensed—and legal—musical performances to take place in Germany were offered simultaneously in Munich and Stuttgart on July 8, 1945. Symphonic concerts were given in Frankfurt and Wiesbaden. Wherever theaters were available or could be improvised, intendants were licensed and aid given in collecting casts and costumes. The find of a large cache of costumes belonging to the Berlin State Opera Company in a salt mine proved a boon to the theater. The costumes were promptly distributed to opera companies throughout Germany.

The first stage performances in the American zone were given in September 1945. In the concert hall of Radio Frankfurt the comedy *Ingeborg* was presented. Munich's Art Theatre launched its first postwar season with a production of *Macbeth*, Kassel's *Staatstheater* followed with Goethe's *Iphigenia auf Tauris*, and Wiesbaden's Deutsches Theater with Goethe's *Die Geschwiester*. In Stuttgart, *Orpheus and Euridice* and *As You Like It* were presented; in Heidelberg, Moliere's *Der Geizige*; and in Ulm, *The Taming of the Shrew*. In Munich, the *Volkstheater* was making its home in a converted sports hall, counting in its repertoire such plays as *Outward Bound*, and the *Kammerspiele in Schauspielhaus* was playing *Our Town*.

In the American sector of Berlin, two theaters were already playing to big audiences when our troops arrived, one an open-air theater. The most important of the theaters in the American sector of the city—the *Hebbel Theater*— opened on August 13 with the *Dreigroschenoper* in the Brecht-Weill adaptation, later presenting Macbeth and Robert Ardrey's *Thunder Rock*, the first modern American play to be shown in Berlin in years. In Bremen, theatrical productions included Goethe's *Stella*, Ibsen's *Nora*, and Lessing's *Nathan der Weise*, staged by the *Stadtstheater* and several smaller theater companies.

In addition to the state and municipally supported theaters in the principal cities, stage shows were presented in smaller towns by stock companies and variety troupes, all licensed by Military Government. Permanent tax-supported repertory theaters were developing in some towns, attesting to the integral part the theater plays in the lives of Germans of all classes. Theaters and orchestras, like schools, had for many decades been supported by states and municipalities; and private commercial theaters were almost unknown, save for a few in the larger cities such as Berlin, Hamburg and Munich.

A number of theaters accepted American plays for production. Once the German rights to these plays had been secured and adapted for the German stage, the leading producers showed little or no hesitation to stage the best of contemporary American drama.

Plays such as *Thunder Rock, Our Town, Abe Lincoln in Illinois,* and *Uncle Harry* were among the first to be produced—and were well liked. Other plays brought to Germany included *Ah! Wilderness, The Barretts of Wimpole Street, The Skin of Our Teeth, The Time of Your Life, Ethan Frome, Men in White, Angel Street,* and the like.

That which the American Military Government could not achieve in Germany by means of the Hollywood film it achieved by means of the play—but to a smaller audience. The intelligent theater-goer was not slow to appreciate the fundamental humanitarianism of *Lincoln in Illinois* and the universality of themes portrayed by *Ah! Wilderness* and *The Skin of Our Teeth.* Plays by Eugene O'Neill, Thornton Wilder, Robert Sherwood, Elmer Rice, and William Saroyan were much in demand.

Military Government sought the assistance of representatives of German theater unions and independent experts in selecting and approving dramatic and musical artists. The reestablishment of local branches of the old actors' federation— the GDB (*Genossenschaft Deutscher Bünenangehöriger*), founded in 1871 but dissolved by the Nazis, constituted an important activity.

To conform to the over-all policy of turning over to the Germans the direction of the mass media of education, a special examination board, to examine and approve applicants in the theatrical and musical professions, was set up in 1946. Consisting of delegates of the new theater and music unions, representatives of state and city cultural departments, and leading nonprofessional citizens, the board took over functions hitherto carried out by Military Government officers. The board, however, possessed only the power to recommend, final decision being retained by Military Government. At the same time, *Land* governments were allowed to select their own theater intendants for tax-supported institutions, provided they selected men who had previously received Military Government licenses to practice their profession.

Germany was coming into her own again also in the field of symphonic music and opera. Music officers on the staffs of Military Government in each of the *Länder* in the American zone of occupation aided orchestra conductors, musicians, and opera directors and singers in a revival of musical life. Weeding out undesirable artists and managers, finding suitable concert halls and stages for symphony and opera, replacing lost and damaged instruments, and providing music scores, absorbed the attention of these officers in the normal course of their duties.

In spite of difficulties of all sorts and the primitiveness of everyday life, music lovers flocked to the improvised concert hall and opera house. The Munich Philharmonic Orchestra gave its first postwar concert on July 8, 1945 and a chamber music recital played to an overflow audience at the Bavaria State Theater. Frankfurt's musical life started with a memorial concert in honor of the city's dead who had lost their lives in concentration camps. Heidelberg and Wiesbaden followed suit with concerts early in August.

A short four months after the end of hostilities, musical activities were well on their way. Philharmonic orchestras were established in most of the larger cities and smaller orchestras were going concerns in a good many of the towns.

Berlin's famed Philharmonic Orchestra made its home in the American sector of the city—in the Titania Palast, a large motion picture theater used by American troops. Our Military Government music officers in Berlin paid particular attention to this orchestra, promoting its concerts, providing a permanent home for it, establishing a fair wage scale for the musicians, and establishing the organization on a firm financial foundation. The distinguished conductor, Leo Borchard, was the first to head the orchestra under American sponsorship, but after his accidental death in September 1945, the young Roumanian conductor, Sergiu Celibidache, was appointed to lead the orchestra.

Our policy of thorough denazification, especially in the cultural media, prevented the employment of the talents of such famous orchestra conductors as Wilhelm Fürtwangler, who led the Berlin Philharmonic in Hitler days, and headed at the same time the Reich Chamber of Music; Hans Knappertsbusch, conductor of the Bavaria State Opera Orchestra, and Hans Swarowski, conductor in Stuttgart's *Staatstheater*. Concert pianist

Walter Gieseking was prohibited from giving concerts, since he had voluntarily co-operated with the Reich Ministry of Propaganda in furthering Nazi musical programs abroad and had frequently offered his services free to musical events sponsored by the Nazi Party.

Of opera, much was offered in Germany, Military Government giving and providing facilities for the repair of bombed-out opera houses and the construction of improvised ones. Music-loving and music-hungry residents of Frankfurt saw their operas performed on an improvised stage on the floor of the heavily damaged stock exchange, since only the outer shell remained of the elegant permanent opera house. With little technical equipment, such works as *Fidelio, The Marriage of Figaro*, and *Tosca*, were given fine artistic performances, this writer himself having delighted in more than one of them.

In Wiesbaden, opera began with a premiere of *Madame Butterfly*. Munich offered *La Boheme;* Bremen, *Pagliacci* and *Cavaleria Rusticana*, staged in a schoolhouse. In Berlin, the German State Opera Company treated its inhabitants (and occupiers) to some memorable performances of opera and ballet in the Admiralpalast, a theater that served in place of the badly damaged State Opera House, in the Russian sector of the city. The Municipal Opera Company, in the British sector, also gave fine performances. And in the American sector, which could boast no prewar opera house of its own, a local company calling itself the *Kammeroper Bronsgest* gave the first performance of opera in Berlin after the end of the war when it presented Rossini's *Barber of Seville* on August 16, 1945.

The revival of musical life was not confined to the professional arts alone. To counteract the widespread apathy that hung like a pall over Germany, especially over German youth, Military Government initiated the organization of amateur choral societies and youth orchestras, and amateur theatrical groups.

Besides all this, contemporary American music, not available in Germany since 1933, was placed at the disposal of

German orchestras. Among the first works to be performed were Howard Hanson's "Third Symphony," Walter Piston's "The Incredible Flutist," Samuel Barber's "Adagio," and chamber music by Charles Ives.

In Berlin, an inter-Allied music library, for the release throughout Germany of music scores of non-German music was opened in the summer of 1946. It became one of the very few enterprises in which Soviet Russia agreed to co-operate with the Western nations. Originating with American Military Government, the idea was enthusiastically received by the British and later adhered to by the French and Russians. By means of this library, much of the non-German music that had been kept out of Germany under the Third Reich was made available to German audiences, both in concert halls and on the radio. Orchestras in each of the zones of occupation thus found it easy to obtain compositions they wished to perform by borrowing them from the library. An extensive lending service was thereby inaugurated.[3]

In the theater and in music a veritable renaissance was discernible in otherwise devastated and prostrate Germany. Through not a few policy and tactical errors, through a fair share of early "muddling," and amidst a general want of knowledge on the part of the public of the multifariousness of a military occupation and government, much good was done and considerable progress made. Well might the American public be gratified at the work accomplished by its government and the government's representatives in Germany.

---

3. "Inter-Allied Music Library," *Military Government Weekly Information Bulletin*, No. 105 (August 11, 1947), p. 11 ff.

Hill, Russell, *Struggle for Germany*, New York and London, 1947.
    Germany as a world problem in contest between East and West. Emphasis is on life in Berlin. Some reference is made to the public education media.
Jaspers, Karl, *The Question of German Guilt*, New York, 1947.
    A treatise on individual versus collective guilt.
Koch-Weser, Erich, *Hitler and Beyond*, New York, 1945.
    A short survey of modern German history. Includes a discussion of the Germans' postwar state of mind and the problems of enlightenment.
Kris, Ernst and Speier, Hans, *German Radio Propaganda*, London, 1944.
    German radio propaganda on the home front in World War II is discussed in connection with each of the important events of the war, such as the battle of Britain, Stalingrad, etc.
Lilge, Frederic, *The Abuse of Learning*, New York, 1948.
    The catastrophe of German culture is linked to inherent traits in the culture of the whole of the Western world.
Lippmann, Walter, *Public Opinion*, New York, 1922.
    A study of the sources of public opinion and its influence on people's minds.
Lowenstein, Karl, *Hitler's Germany*, New York, 1939.
    A survey of the governmental structure of the Third Reich and the Nazi instruments of political power.
Mander, A. L., *Foundations of Modern World Society*, Stanford, California and London, 1947.
    A general work on the history of international organization, containing references to some of the cultural media and their place in international intercourse.
Manthey-Zorn, Otto, *Germany in Travail*, Boston, 1922.
    The story of Germany's spiritual struggle after World War I.
Margolin, Leo J., *Paper Bullets: A Brief History of Psychological Warfare in World War II*.
    A survey of the history of psychological warfare in western Europe and development of a case for a government department of information.
May, Mark A., *A Social Psychology of War and Peace*, New Haven, 1943.
    Develops the thesis that the desire to make war is not inherent; it is socially acquired.

McMurry, Ruth E., *The Cultural Approach*, Chapel Hill, N. C., 1947.
A cultural approach is recommended to international understanding and cooperation.

Morgenthau, Jr., Henry, *Germany is Our Problem*, New York and London, 1945.
A formulation of the treatment to be accorded Germany after the war, by the leading proponent of the "hard peace" school.

Neumann, Franz, *Behemoth*, New York and London, 1942.
A work on the structure and practice of National Socialism.

Padover, Saul K., *Experiment in Germany*, New York, 1946.
Personal experiences of a psychological warfare officer in Germany.

Pollock, James K., *Germany Under Occupation*, Ann Arbor, Mich., 1947.
A collection of basic Military Government laws and directives.

Price, H. and Schorske, C. E., *The Problem of Germany*, New York, 1947.
The authors discuss the general problem of German reconstruction. Make brief comments on ideological reorientation.

*The Psychological Warfare Division, SHAEF*, Bad Homburg, Germany, 1945.
A detailed study of psychological warfare operations conducted by Supreme Headquarters, Allied Expeditionary Force.

Rodnick, David, *Postwar Germans*, New Haven, 1948.
A study of German social life by an anthropologist with the Information Control staff of Military Government.

Röpke, W., *The Solution of the German Problem*, New York, 1947
An analysis of the German national character. A distinction is made between leaders and led.

Seger, G. H. and Marck, S. K., *Germany: To Be or Not To Be?* New York, 1943.
A polemic on collective guilt viewed in the light of Germany's history.

Stolper, Gustav, *German Realities*, New York, 1948.
A general survey of German problems by one who served on the Hoover fact-finding mission to Germany in the winter of 1947.

Stowe, Leland, *Nazi Means War*, New York, 1934.

A journalist's view of National Socialism and the German people.

Vansittart, Lord Robert, *Bones of Contention*, New York, 1945.
A work stressing Germany's incurable menace to the peace of Europe.

Warburg, James P., *Unwritten Treaty*, New York, 1946.
The problem of information in the postwar world as a means of bringing about international understanding.

White, L. and Leigh, R. D., *Peoples Speaking to Peoples*, Chicago, 1946.
A discussion of the media of mass communication and a recommendation for a United States information program abroad.

Zink, Harold, *American Military Government in Germany*, New York, 1947.
A general survey of Military Government functions and organization.

## ARTICLES

Almond, G. A., "The German Resistance Movement," *Current History*, X (May 1946), 409-19.

Baukhage, "What Germany is Reading," *Saturday Review of Literature*, XXIX (February 23, 1946), 5 ff.

Biggs, John A., "Hollywood in Bavaria," *Information Bulletin, Magazine of U. S. Military Government*, No. 128 (February 10, 1948), 6-7.

Brailsford, H. N., "The Re-education of Germany," *Contemporary Review*, CLXVIII (August 1945), 70-75.

Brooks, Paul, "Books Follow the Jeep," *Publishers' Weekly*, CXLVII (December 8, 1945), 2528-30.

Carr, W. G., "Postwar Education in Enemy Countries," *The Public Opinion Quarterly*, VIII (1944-45), 17-22.

Cramer, F. H., "The Re-education of Germany: An American Experiment," *Forum*, CIV (October 1945), 114-19.

Daniell, Raymond, " 'We Talk Tough, But We Act Soft,' " *New York Times Magazine*, (October 7, 1945), 5 ff.

Davies, Harriet E., "Germany Can Be Changed," *Independent Woman*, XXIV (January 1945), 9 ff.

Dent, Edward J., "Music and Drama in Germany," *The Contemporary Review*, CLXX (October 1945), 215-19.

"Gentle Swing for Germans," *Newsweek*, XXVI (August 2, 1945), 89-90.

Gurian, Waldemar, "Re-educating Germany," *Commonweal*, XLVIII, (August 27, 1948), 466-69.

Hale, William Harlan, "Our Failure in Germany," *Harper's Magazine*, CXCI (December 1945), 515-23.

Hale, William Harlan, "General Clay—On His Own," *Harper's Magazine*, CXCVII (December 1948), 86-94.

Hermens, F. A., "The Danger of Stereotypes in Viewing Germany," *The Public Opinion Quarterly*, IX (1945), 418-27.

Hill, Gladwin, "Allied-Soviet Unity Lacking On Germans' Re-education," *New York Times*, May 26, 1946.

Hirsch, Felix E., "The German Press, Yesterday and Tomorrow," *Current History*, IX (August 1945), 104-11.

"Inter-Allied Music Library," *Weekly Information Bulletin, Magazine of U. S. Military Government* No. 105 (August 11, 1947), 11-12.

Jacobs, Harry A., "Education by Radio," *Information Bulletin, Magazine of U. S. Military Government in Germany*, No. 151 (December 28, 1948), 9 ff.

Kirkpatrick, Clifford, "Sociological Principles and Occupied Germany," *American Sociological Review*, XI (1946), 67-78.

Lehmann-Haupt, H. "German Publishing Begins to Revive," *Publishers' Weekly*, CXLIX (March 16, 1946), 1617-18.

Lehmann-Haupt, H., "The German Book Trade in 1945, Part II," *Publishers' Weekly*, CXLVIII (December 8, 1945), 2531-33.

Lehmann-Haupt, H., "German Publishing Begins to Revive," III," *Publishers' Weekly*, CXLVIII (December 22, 1945), 2684-86.

Lowrey, L. G., "To Make the Germans Men of Peace," *New York Times Magazine*, (June 17, 1945), 12 ff.

Middleton, Drew, "Only a Start in Re-educating Germans," *New York Times Magazine*, (March 31, 1946), 10 ff.

Neumann, Franz L., "Re-educating the Germans," *Commentary*, III (June 1947), 517-25.

Pollard, John A., "Words Are Cheaper than Blood," *The Public Opinion Quarterly*, IX (1945), 283-304.

"Problems Confronting Publications Control in Germany," *Publishers' Weekly*, CLI (March 25, 1947), 1788-91.

Reichmann, F., "The First Year of American Publications Control in Germany," *Publishers' Weekly*, CL (November 16, 1946), 2810-12.

Riess, Curt, "We Must Win Another Battle in Germany," *New York Times Magazine*, (May 20, 1945), 5 ff.

Russell, W. F., "Teaching Germans to Teach Themselves," *Foreign Affairs*, XXVII (October 1948), 69-77.

Sageser, A. B., "Military Occupation of the Confederate States,"

*Current History*, IX (September 1945), 227-34.

Sibert, Brig. General Edwin L., "The German Mind: Our Greatest Problem," *New York Times Magazine*, (February 17, 1946), 7 ff.

Sollmann, W. F., "The German Press After V-Day," *The Public Opinion Quarterly* VIII (1944-45), 537-43.

Stagner, Ross, "Opinions of Psychologists on Peace Planning," *The Journal of Psychology*, XIX (1945), 3-16

Wanger, Walter, "OWI and Motion Pictures," *The Public Opinion Quarterly*, VII (1943-44), 100-110.

West, R., "The Psychology of Peace-Making," *Fortnightly*, CLXII (December, 1944), 357-63.

Williams, F. W., "German Opinion and American Isolationism," *The Public Opinion Quarterly*, XI (1947), 179-188.

Youngren, Ingrid, "U. S. Drama in Germany," *Information Bulletin, Magazine of U. S. Military Government in Germany*, No. 150 (December 14, 1948), 5-8.

Ziemer, Gregor, "Our Educational Failure in Germany," *The American Mercury*, LXII (June 1946), 726-33.

Zink, Harold, "A Political Scientist Looks at Military Government in the European Theater of Operations," *The American Political Science Review*, XL (December 1946), 1097-1112.

NEWSPAPERS

New York *Times*, December 21, 1918; April 24, 1945; May 11, 1945; May 16, 1945; May 26, 1945.

## KEY TO ABBREVIATIONS USED IN FOOTNOTES

ICD—Information Control Division.
ODIC — Office of the Director of Information Control.
OMGUS — Office of Military Government for Germany (U. S.).
USFET — Headquarters United States Forces European Theater.